"And What About College?"

How homeschooling leads to admissions to the best colleges and universities

Revised Second Edition

Holt/GWS

Published by Holt Associates, Inc.
2380 Massachusetts Ave, Suite 104
Cambridge, MA 02140

Original cover art by Maria Whitworth

First printing 1997
Second printing 1/98
Third printing 6/99
Fourth printing 9/99
Second edition 4/2000
Printed in the United States of America by
McNaughton & Gunn, Ltd., Ann Arbor, Michigan.

Library of Congress Cataloging-in-Publication Data

Cohen, Cafi
  And what about college?: how homeschooling leads to admissions to the best
  colleges and universities.—Rev. 2nd ed.
       p.cm.
    Includes bibliographical references and index.
  ISBN 0-913677-11-6
    1. Home schooling—United States. 2. College choice—United States. 3.
  Universities and colleges—United States–Admission. I.Title.
  LC40.C64 2000
  371.04'2—dc21

                                                                    00-029589

TABLE OF CONTENTS

ACKNOWLEDGMENTS

To homeschool our children, we merely crossed over bridges built by others. My family owes so much to those early homeschooling families and advocates who wrote about their experiences, among them John Holt, David and Micki Colfax, Raymond and Dorothy Moore, Mary Pride, plus the staff and countless contributors associated with *Home Education Magazine* and *Growing Without Schooling*.

Second, I will always be indebted to Kathy Claus and Carol Cynova and their families in New Mexico for giving freely of their time and serving as our original homeschooling mentors. Where would we be without people like this? In Colorado, Peggy McKibben gets credit for providing a place for me to do the original workshops that led to this book.

Thanks also to Mark and Helen Hegener for initially believing in this project and to Patrick Farenga and the *Growing Without Schooling* staff for seeing it through and encouraging me to write a second edition. Patrick Farenga, homeschooling mother Terri Endsley, and my husband Terrell Cohen have made valuable contributions to this second edition.

For the original book's content, I am indebted to several members of the Prodigy Old Timers Club, especially Richard Shalvoy, the encourager; Melissa Heeren, book titler; Karl Bunday, resident intellectual; Kay Crowley, Webmeister extraordinaire; the late Jim Jackson, ultimate arbitrator of common sense; and Domi O'Brien, who educated me about unusual ways to obtain college credit. Currently, I draw many new ideas from the marvelous homeschooling contributors to the Kaleidoscapes online bulletin boards, which would not exist without the tireless efforts of Cindy Johns.

I owe a belated thank you to the thousands of homeschooling parents and teenagers who have attended my workshops nationwide as well as to those who read the first edition. My gratitude extends also to hundreds of parents who have written me after reading my columns in *Home Education Magazine, Homeschooling Today,* and The LINK. Your questions and comments have driven the content of this revised edition.

I have received valuable comments and editorial assistance from David and Micki Colfax, Patrick Farenga, Judy Alexander, John and Dolores Fischer, Carol Wetherill, Richard Freeman, Sean Hill, Kathleen Julicher, Susan Sato, Judith Allee, Jeffrey Cohen, Tamara Cohen, and Terrell Cohen, my husband, who read more drafts than anyone else.

Finally, none of this would have been possible without my immediate family. My daughter Tamara was always willing to try new things and at the same time gave counter-evidence to those who claim homeschoolers are inadequately socialized. My son Jeff's pursuit of his interests showed how much homeschoolers can accomplish in relatively little time. My husband Terry has supported all of us in our endeavors, from when we began homeschooling to writing this book. I am grateful to all three for the wonderful years that we homeschooled and for their continuing support.

Cafi Cohen
Arroyo Grande, California
10 January 2000

PREFACE

Steven Covey, the author of *Seven Habits of Highly Effective People*, says, "Begin with the end in mind." I wish we had. Our path would have been clearer and smoother. We would have approached the college application process with more confidence, and perhaps—who knows—with even greater success. I hope that this book helps more homeschooling families begin with the end in mind.

Introduction

When we first published this book in 1997 there was still anxiety as to whether homeschooling could actually lead to college admissions. Certainly there were high profile college admissions and success stories to encourage and inspire homeschoolers, such as the Colfax family, whose boys got scholarships to Harvard and Yale, or Rebecca Sealfon, the homeschooler who won the national spelling bee. But parents of "ordinary children" want to be reassured and shown that their homeschooled children can also get into college, and Cafi's book has served as a practical guide and inspiration for thousands of families seeking this help.

The Wall Street Journal reported in a front page story (2/11/2000) about the success of homeschoolers getting into the colleges of their choice: "As the movement grows larger and more diverse, evidence is mounting that homeschooling, once confined to the political and religious fringe, has achieved results not only on par with public education, but in some ways surpassing it. Though homeschooling may never be feasible for most families, the data offer little comfort to those who advocate a standardized curriculum as the best hope for improving American education. After all, each home-based pupil follows a unique lesson plan." Thoroughly revised, updated and with new sections added, *"And What About College?"* is a book for anyone with a non-traditional background seeking college admissions, not just homeschoolers.

An important issue that Cafi touches on, and is an important subject that I hope to see many more books printed about in the future, is whether or not four years of college is indeed the right choice for all young people. The assumption of most educators is that children must go to college in order to complete their educations (I firmly disagree with this notion since no one's education is ever complete in my mind. We continue learning throughout our lives). However, as homeschooling clearly demonstrates, there are more ways to learn and grow than by completing conventional curricula in traditional schools.

The growing numbers of people who participate in adult education courses, in business seminars, in on-the-job training, and in internet, video, correspondence, and other types of independent study programs, are quickly transforming the educational opportunities that have been the norm for the twentieth century. The new millenium offers many opportunities for learning to be individualized and focused on specific skills or personal development, rather than on broad, general educational goals chosen by committees that claim to know what everyone needs to know now and in the future. Cafi's book is about how you can fit in to today's college admission process, but it also points to the future and the many issues education faces in the twenty-first century that are being addressed by homeschoolers now.

I think this book can also be used by homeschoolers not planning to go to college, or young adults who have left school without degrees, to prove to prospective employers that they are capable of doing or learning "the job"—since Cafi provides a sound framework for assessing one's strengths, addressing weaknesses as needed, and presenting it all on paper. For all these reasons, I urge you to read this story and study the appendices to learn how Cafi's children got into college without schooling.

Patrick Farenga
Publisher
Cambridge, MA

CHAPTER I

OUR STORY

In the spring of 1993, our homeschooled son Jeff won an appointment to the United States Air Force Academy. What a thrill—both for him and for us. We knew other elite colleges and universities had accepted homeschoolers. But we never knew until then if we, too, would succeed.

Jeff also gained admission to the United States Naval Academy, Boston University, and the University of Colorado at Boulder. West Point put him on their waiting list. Jeff won substantial scholarship offers from Army, Navy, and Air Force Reserve Officer Training Corps (ROTC). After he received these offers, half a dozen other colleges actively recruited him. Two of these schools, Vanderbilt University in Tennessee and Rensselaer Polytechnic Institute in New York, offered Jeff full scholarships.

More recently our homeschooled daughter Tamara received acceptances from two selective colleges, Agnes Scott College in Georgia and Stephens College in Missouri. Emory University in Georgia placed her on their waiting list. With her slightly-above-average Scholastic Aptitude Test (SAT) score, making the waiting list at this selective institution was a triumph. Tamara chose Agnes Scott College, which she attended on a substantial merit scholarship.

Talk about hands-on learning experiences. We survived high school homeschooling. With few guidelines, we succeeded with college admissions. Perhaps years of homeschooling—figuring things out on our own and finding assistance in the larger community—prepared us.

We began homeschooling in the late 1980's. Jeff was a seventh grader and Tamara a sixth grader at "the best middle school in Albuquerque, New Mexico," to which we had recently moved.

Terrell, my husband, was a dentist in the United States Air Force. As part of a military family, Jeff and Tamara had attended school in three other states—California, North Dakota, and Texas. The New Mexico middle school promised to be just another educational institution where we would all learn another set of ropes.

Jeff and Tamara, at that point, looked like children who had everything going for them. Each had a full schedule of gifted and honors classes in addition to the typical roster of extracurricular activities. Both took piano lessons. They played on basketball and baseball teams, and they swam competitively in the summer. They got along well with their peers. When asked about school, both our children were likely to say, "It's okay," without elaborating. They didn't love it, nor did they hate it.

I was concerned that Jeff and Tamara did not view school more positively. I worried also about academics. Although both children received good report cards, sometimes it seemed that their abilities did not warrant the high grades. My straight-A's-in-math daughter would hesitate when I asked her to multiply six times seven. Jeff did not enjoy recreational reading. Neither child seemed to be on track to becoming a self-directed learner.

Instead, Jeff and Tamara had learned to play the game. They turned in work on time and cooperated with class activities. They listened to the teacher. Most significantly, they were not discipline problems. Several of their teachers had told me over the years that disorderly behavior predominated in most classrooms. Mere decorum earned not just a passing grade, but an "A" or a "B." Jeff and Tamara had years of report cards with "A's" and "B's" on them. What did those grades really mean? Had our children mastered anything?

Accidentally one day, I heard a homeschooling family interviewed on a television talk show. Never thinking we would actually homeschool, I mentioned the topic at dinner, just as something interesting to discuss. As I described the homeschooling family and their activities, both Jeff and Tamara listened intently. After a couple of questions and a short discussion, both said they wanted to try homeschooling. As the eager-to-get-to-it pre-teenagers they were, they wanted us to begin the very next day.

Whoa! Here were two children who did well in school, yet home-schooling looked attractive to them. As I began questioning them closely about their reasons, I heard the words "waste of time" and "silly" and "pointless" over and over. School bored them.

We were hesitant to make any changes. After all, both Jeff and Tamara had pretty paper trails (good grades, positive teacher recommendations, high standardized test scores). Additionally, my husband and I had a long list of questions. Where would we find curriculum and other materials? How would homeschooling mesh with my attending school and teaching piano part-time? Were others homeschooling in our vicinity? How could we find them? Could our children return to school at any time? What were the legal implications?

Library research and talking to local home educators took care of most of our questions about homeschooling. Most helpful was David & Micki Colfax's *Homeschooling For Excellence*. Our hesitancy about home education completely disappeared after I spent two days—one for each child—observing everything in their public school classes. I often now advise any parent waffling between homeschooling and continued public schooling to do the same, to visit school and simply listen.

As I said, I observed for two full days. I did not help out. I listened and I watched. During those days, I kept track of administrative time versus on-task time. Administrative time includes passing out supplies, making announcements, taking roll, distributing supplies, forming groups, and disciplining (the biggest time waster of all). On-task time is roughly defined as really doing something: reading, writing, discussing issues, working problems, listening to a lecture, watching a demonstration, or participating in an activity.

The two days I attended, on-task time each day totaled less than one hour. Less than one hour out of six. It was appalling. Students engaged in academic activities less than twenty percent of each school day. It made the building look more like a warehouse or processing facility than a learning center. Teachers spent most of each class period on administrative concerns. I learned later that this particular school was not unusual.

How could we do any worse? Even if our homeschooling was very basic and simple—say working our way through math texts and reading a lot—our children would accomplish more than if they stayed in school. Even though we had much to learn about home education, we decided we had little to lose and perhaps a lot to gain.

So we embarked on the homeschooling adventure. In 1988, with both the children beginning middle school, thoughts of college were far off. Each year, Jeff and Tamara had the option of returning to school. In fact, we initially expected that they would return to school. Surely high school had to be better? College was not among our concerns.

Each year, we put together an eclectic curriculum (see examples in Appendix E). We built our homeschooling program around our students' interests and goals, and we used a variety of approaches and resources. These included traditional materials (texts); unit studies (in-depth, thematic projects); outside activities (4-H, sports, music, church); and volunteer and paying jobs. In addition, we scheduled substantial time for student-directed studies and activities (termed unschooling by some). From the beginning, Jeff and Tamara collaborated in planning their homeschooling.

Traditionalists say children learn best with texts, schedules, and exams. Unit study proponents say children learn best with thematic hands-on activities. And unschoolers say children learn best when their interests direct the learning. Eclectic home educators, in contrast, say there is no one way that all children learn best all the time. Instead of implementing a particular educational philosophy, we focused on each child. We changed methods and materials on an as-needed basis. When something was not working, we looked for alternatives. With our son's and daughter's reading and basic math skills in place, we emphasized learning how to learn and using community resources. Within our comfort level, we let our children's interests direct their learning.

Each year, both Jeff and Tamara decided to continue homeschooling. Their reasons were as individual as their personalities. Jeff saw school as a colossal waste of time. He turned out, eventually, to be more correct about the efficiency of home education than any of us originally guessed. He completed high school a year and a half ahead of schedule and concurrently accumulated more than twenty college credits. Tamara was and is more people-oriented. She liked having time and flexibility to engage in more community activities than full-time school attendance would have allowed. Over the years, she held many volunteer and paying jobs.

As Jeff's high school years approached, we seriously re-evaluated having him return to school. At this point, he knew that he wanted to attend the United States Air Force Academy and eventually train to fly jets. Still in Albuquerque, we investigated conditions at the local high school down the street. After spending an entire day there, Jeff emphatically said that he wanted to continue homeschooling. Government school still looked like a waste of time to me, too.

We were in a quandary. The Air Force Academy has a conservative reputation. How would they react to an application from a student who homeschooled through high school? What would they think of our non-traditional methods? Had they ever before seen a home-schooled applicant?

Jeff and I decided to co-author a letter to Academy officials. We wrote and told them of Jeff's interest—both in attending the Academy and in continuing homeschooling. We briefly explained the benefits of home education. And we asked them to comment specifically on three courses of action: (1) return to government school; (2) homeschool high school using an accredited independent-study course; and (3) homeschool high school by putting together our own materials, as we had been doing.

I expected that they would give a thumbs-up to option number one and possibly to number two. I never anticipated that they would comment favorably on option number three, that we continue homeschooling just as we had been. The response surprised us all. They stated that each of the three options was equally acceptable. The second half of the letter emphasized that Jeff should participate in a physical conditioning program. Most encouragingly, they told us that the Air Force Academy had admitted two to four homeschoolers per year for the past several years.

Thus Jeff and eventually Tamara became high school home-schoolers. They both completed traditional high school work with American School, an independent-study institution now near Chicago, in Lansing, Illinois. Because of American School's no-nonsense approach, they spent less than two hours daily with textbooks. They devoted most of their time to their own projects and activities.

When Fall 1992 rolled around, we knew it was time to think about Jeff's college applications. We had voluminous documentation of his accomplishments. Our records included award certificates, medals, trophies, letters of recommendation, transcripts from colleges and correspondence schools, piano recital programs, work samples, diving team practice schedules, church youth group activity calendars, copies of Civil Air Patrol newsletter contributions, photos, flying logs, an FCC Amateur Radio License, standardized test scores, and more.

It was all in a big folder labeled "Jeff". Unfortunately, except for attendance records we were required to keep by law, that folder was the sum total of our homeschool record keeping. We knew Jeff had received excellent preparation for almost any college in the nation. He had already proven he could succeed with college-level courses. We debated how to put it all together into a clean, concise, easy-to-understand format. How could we best appeal to admissions officers at selective colleges?

We were aware that universities and colleges nationwide had accepted homeschooled students (see Appendix F). We had few specifics on exactly how they had gone about it, though. In one sense, that was good. Starting from scratch forced us to think carefully about what we submitted and how we presented it.

By trial and error, we settled on three information-organizing tools:

- Cover letter

- Home-brew transcript

- Résumé

Most college applications do not specifically request these documents. But we found that using them simplified homeschooling record keeping and facilitated application review. Out of nine applications to nine different colleges plus submissions to numerous scholarship programs, not one reviewer asked us additional questions about what we sent. No one asked us to further justify or document our homeschooling. Since the first edition of this book, hundreds of families, adapting our format to their situations, have written and reported similar success with college admissions.

The cover letter, home-brew transcript, and résumé worked well for us. As detailed later, these three information-organizing tools document a variety of homeschooling methods. They work for those using a traditional approach. They work equally well for unschoolers, those building their homeschooling completely around the student's interests and goals. They work for everyone in between—classical principle approach home educators, unit study fans, and others. And they work for those who take college courses concurrent with high school homeschooling.

The remainder of this book is based on my homeschooling workshops and on comments and questions from home educators who read the first edition of *"And What About College?"* This new edition reflects both the concerns of families homeschooling teenagers in the new millennium as well as rapidly changing college admissions policies.

The following chapters discuss high school at home, researching colleges, keeping records, writing transcripts, assembling college applications, and college at home. The final chapter answers commonly asked questions. Appendices are chock-full of information, including copies of the transcripts we used.

Even though our transcripts, cover letters, and résumés led to admission to our children's first-choice colleges, I urge you not to copy them exactly. Why? You will do a better job if you read about our process and change it to fit your student. Please do not read this book as a how-to title. Instead, think of it as an example of something that worked only because we customized documentation to our son and daughter. It is a bag of tricks, some of which may fit your situation, some not. Always customize your homeschooling, your records, and your college applications according to your student's interests and goals. Be selective. Take what you can use, and leave the rest.

CHAPTER II

THE GOOD NEWS

Getting In

Many colleges do not advertise a fact that many of their catalogs state in different words, namely that admission is a slam-dunk. Indeed, it is more difficult to get a driver's license in many states than to win admission to a majority of colleges and universities nationwide. We all buy into the Harvard hype: college admission is difficult to impossible—at all colleges. Not true. Yes, Harvard is very competitive. They only admit top applicants. But while Harvard, Princeton and Stanford carefully review and screen applications, a majority of private four-year colleges and many state universities practice near-open admissions. They accept almost everyone, regardless of academic background. They may require an SAT score, but they do not exclude anybody with a low score. Similarly, most community and junior colleges—more than 1,000 two-year associate-degree-granting schools in the United States—have open admissions policies.

Many four-year colleges and universities, over 1,000 in number nationwide, are either non-competitive or only marginally competitive. According to Barron's *Profiles of American Colleges,* more than 75% of schools accept 75-99% of students who apply. In other words, most schools granting bachelor's degrees admit most applicants.

Barron's classifies schools as non-competitive or less competitive or competitive, in contrast to those that are very competitive, highly competitive, or most competitive. Throughout the remainder of this book, I use the words "less selective" or "non-selective" for schools that accept 75-99% of applicants. I reserve the term "selective" for those colleges and universities in Barron's very competitive, highly competitive, or most competitive categories, those colleges that accept less than 75% of applicants.

Excellent colleges fall into the non-selective and less selective categories: Baylor University, Texas; Embry-Riddle Aeronautical University, Arizona; University of California at Santa Barbara, California; Youngstown State University, Ohio; University of Bridgeport, Connecticut; to name a few. With good documentation, homeschoolers with average academic backgrounds and standardized test scores will have little trouble gaining admission.

Selective colleges and universities, numbering 300-350 nationwide, do pick and choose, accepting anywhere from 10% to 75% of those applying. Examples are Harvard University, Massachusetts; Rice University, Texas; Rose-Hulman Institute of Technology, Indiana; University of California at Berkeley, California; and Emory University, Georgia.

Since the early 1980's, homeschooled students have won admission to a wide range of colleges and universities. And the list of selective schools that have accepted homeschoolers continues to grow (see Appendix F). If your student applies to one of these institutions, he probably will not be the first homeschooler, either to apply or to be admitted.

Sean Callaway, a homeschooling father and professional admissions counselor, works primarily with underprivileged youth in New York City. He points out: "Home education is a hot topic among professional admissions people because every one is trying to maximize the number of... students who enroll, but few know how to open lines of communication with home educated students." Keep this in mind. Admissions officers want to talk to homeschooled students, and most do not know how to reach you.

Slowly, however, college personnel are learning how to reach homeschoolers. Some institutions advertise in publications like *Home Education Magazine, Growing Without Schooling, Homeschooling Today,* and *Practical Homeschooling.* Pennsylvania State University offers a Home Schooling High Schoolers' Conference. I counted admissions representatives from two to six colleges at each of six homeschool conferences in the spring of 1999. At college fairs, admissions representatives encourage applications from homeschooled students. Several colleges, like Nyack College in New York and Bellhaven College in Mississippi, even offer scholarships earmarked for homeschooled applicants.

User-Friendly College Admissions and Programs

Traditionally, applying to college involves filling out a lengthy application and submitting supporting documentation like transcripts, standardized test scores, and letters of recommendation. Increasingly, however, homeschooled students and others are exploring alternatives. One of these alternatives is back-door college entrance.

With back-door admissions, the student simply enrolls in one or more college classes as a non-degree-seeking student. He completes basic forms, skipping the lengthy admissions application, transcripts of previous work, and standardized test scores. After a semester or two, the student, using successfully completed college classes as the basis for his application, petitions for admission to a degree-granting program at the school. The advantage for homeschoolers is obvious. Students admitted through the back-door process avoid writing high school transcripts or compiling portfolios.

A second alternative involves completing college-at-home in a distance learning, independent study format. Most homeschoolers certainly have the experience to succeed with such an endeavor. Younger teenagers ready for college-level work also find this an appealing option.

Alexandra Swann, a New Mexico homeschooler, completed high school studies at age 11. Using independent study college programs, she received her bachelor's degree at age 15 and her master's degree at age 16. She recounts her experience in the book, *No Regrets: How Homeschooling Earned Me A Master's Degree At Age 16*. I explore college-

11

at-home and taking independent-study college courses concurrent with high school in Chapter VIII.

During their high school years, homeschoolers may also earn college credit at home via the College Level Examination Program (CLEP). CLEP tests cover more than 30 different subject areas like chemistry, English Literature, and American Government. More than 2,000 colleges and universities nationwide convert passing scores into college credit. Large bookstores usually stock CLEP study guides, which contain information about how to register for the tests; Appendix J includes contact information for CLEP tests. Always check with your preferred colleges to determine if CLEP scores are accepted.

Similarly, many institutions give college credit and advanced placement in college courses for Advanced Placement (AP) test scores of three or four or better on a five-point scale (see Appendix J). Like CLEP tests, AP tests are subject-specific (for example, Chemistry, French, World History). Preparation materials and registration information are available at most large bookstores. Again, check with individual colleges to learn if they give AP credit.

Something For Everyone

Homeschoolers are a diverse bunch. Some seek colleges that offer flexible programs such as student-devised majors. Some avoid lock-step, graded, text-based education. Others require traditional academic environments in conservative settings. Still others seek programs that emphasize hands-on learning and internships.

Fortunately, there is something for everyone. Programs at various colleges and universities offer alternatives attractive to homeschoolers of every educational philosophy. Examples are co-op programs (half academic, half work experience); student-devised majors; block plans (one subject at a time, in depth); no-grade, portfolio-only courses; and much more. Appendix G lists examples of some of these schools.

The Homeschooling Edge

Are there advantages in applying to college as a homeschooler? Yes. Absolutely. With their uncommon educational backgrounds, homeschoolers stand out from the crowd. Rarity also draws attention. In 1999, homeschoolers comprise approximately one percent of high school students, thus (roughly) about one percent of college applicants.

Most significantly, homeschooling often results in eye-catching accomplishments. When admissions officers examine a home-schooled student's application, they see more than just another teenager with good test scores, decent grades, and the standard list of high school activities.

Instead, they often find themselves reviewing the application of an entrepreneur, a published author, a community volunteer, a musical prodigy, an airplane pilot, or an athlete. Perhaps they will read about a computer whiz, world traveler, multi-linguist, political campaign worker, or house-builder. Atypical activities—not related to typical high school subjects and programs—get the attention of admissions officers.

Yes, high school homeschoolers participate in a wide range of uncommon extracurriculars. Furthermore, in their transcripts and portfolios, they often include non-traditional, attention-getting school subjects that reflect personal interests. Examples are: Greek, Veterinary Medicine, Church History, Tae Kwon Do, Personal Conditioning and Fitness, Rocketry, Music Composition, and Electronics.

Why is an unconventional educational background an advantage in the admissions process? Michele Hernandez, a former Dartmouth College admissions officer, addressed this point in her book, *A Is For Admission*. She says, admissions officers notice activities that say, "Learning excites this student." Additionally, admissions officers seek evidence of "depth of commitment and leadership." Pursuing unusual topics and activities—beyond English and Algebra II and American

13

History and yearbook staff and class treasurer—demonstrates excitement and commitment.

Second, within limits, admissions officers are working to create "A Well-Rounded Student Body." Admissions personnel assemble a well-rounded student body not necessarily by accepting a roster of well-rounded students, but instead by admitting applicants with diverse backgrounds. Homeschooled students who pursue unusual subjects and activities can be very attractive. They enrich and enliven any student body, thereby increasing any university's diversity quotient.

Even though the word "homeschooling" no longer draws blank stares, many admissions representatives have had limited experience with homeschooled applicants. Interestingly, most college admissions officers welcome contact with homeschoolers, probably due to market pressures. Sean Callaway, the independent college admissions counselor mentioned earlier, predicts a big shake-out in the next 15-20 years: "Right now, there are 3600+ institutions of higher education. By year 2010-2015, there will probably be less than 2,000." Homeschoolers can take advantage of this buyer's market.

I confirmed Mr. Callaway's impressions by speaking with hundreds of college admissions workers at college fairs. I have yet to find one negatively biased with respect to homeschooled students. The bias is either non-existent (neutral, they do not know what to make of it) or, more often now in the year 2000, positive (they have had good experience with homeschoolers).

An example is Grove City College, a selective school in western Pennsylvania. In 1994-1995, Grove City College admitted 45% of those who applied. That same year they accepted ten out of twelve homeschooled applicants. An admissions officer at Carleton College in Minnesota said that homeschoolers had a very good track record at their school. She added that, in general, homeschooled students impressed her with their level of motivation and independence.

The University of Denver also has good experience with homeschoolers. Our son, Jeff, applied to one of their high school summer programs called "The Making Of An Engineer." According to the admissions officer, they had 180 applicants for 60 spaces in the college-credit class. He told me he filled the first 30 slots with students who had sky-high standardized test scores. Jeff did not fit into this category. That left 150 applicants for the remaining 30 slots. The admissions officer told us that Jeff got one of those 30 places because he was a homeschooler. Their experience told them that—all other things being equal—homeschooled students would do a better job.

The "S" Word And Other Concerns

Some admissions personnel do express concerns, the biggest one being the "S" word—socialization. Several colleges indicated that they like to see evidence of group activities on homeschoolers' applications. An admissions officer at Rice University emphasized the importance of homeschoolers fully describing their participation in community activities. He said, "...simply reporting homeschool academics creates a weak application."

Other concerns range from documenting academics to obtaining unbiased evaluations of the student's accomplishments. As detailed later in this book, homeschooling families provide evidence of academic achievement in two ways: writing a home-brew transcript or compiling a portfolio. Alternatively, homeschool academics can be documented by an umbrella school (private schools that keep records and generate transcripts for homeschoolers). In either case, letters of recommendation and standardized test scores round out the application to provide unbiased evaluations.

While a few admissions officers prefer external transcripts (transcripts from umbrella or independent-study schools), most admissions officers say they do not care one way or the other. They prefer good documentation, regardless of the source. Students targeting certain colleges should ask early (before beginning grade nine) if an external transcript would be viewed more favorably.

College Admissions Policies

An increase in the homeschooling population coupled with more families home educating teenagers has multiplied the number of homeschooled college applicants in the last five years. Colleges and universities—in increasing numbers—have reacted by writing policies to help them counsel and evaluate homeschooled applicants.

Not all colleges have policies. Some, like the University of Virginia as of 1997, have decided not to write separate policies. They say that having a policy specifically for homeschoolers is inconsistent with their educational philosophy.

At those schools without specific policies for homeschoolers, admissions representatives generally say that they review applications from homeschooled students on a case-by-case basis. Usually, this ensures homeschoolers get individual attention and careful consideration, even at large schools.

Better than the individual attention, though, absence of a policy gives families latitude with respect to the application format. Just as they have customized homeschooling to fit their educational philosophy and their student's interests and goals, families can tailor application documentation to focus on the student's strengths.

Individualizing a college application is both a challenge and an opportunity. One admissions officer at Rice University encourages homeschoolers to make the most of the application process. He welcomes in-depth descriptions of special projects, different lifestyles, and non-academic interests.

Of course, there are exceptions to any rule. Lack of admissions policies for dealing with homeschoolers may be an impediment at one type of institution. Some large state universities and colleges review applicants strictly according to numbers. They rank students according to grade point averages and standardized test scores. The sheer volume of applications precludes in-depth review.

An example is California Polytechnic Institute, in San Luis Obispo. According to their admissions officer, students without four years of high school grades and a standard list of typical high school courses will not be considered for admission. Nothing else will fit into their state-mandated formulas.

Despite the problems, state colleges and universities do admit homeschooled applicants. Homeschoolers who successfully negotiate the application process at state schools usually have acceptable standardized test scores and home-brew or external transcripts with calculated grade point averages.

Think, "Play the game." First, talk to admissions personnel and ask how much the college relies on formulas. To generate the numbers, compile a transcript that includes grades, credits, and a grade point average (see Chapter V). Alternatively, consider using an umbrella school like Clonlara in Michigan or an independent-study school, like American School in Illinois, for the transcript.

What about those colleges and universities that have policies? First of all, the policies exist in several forms. Some are internal memos. Others are form letters to homeschooling applicants. Some are public documents anyone can read on the Internet. Others, like those for Georgia state colleges, have been written into state law.

Always ask if a college or university of interest has written policies for evaluating and admitting for homeschoolers. Do this when your homeschooler is in grade eight or nine, if possible. Admissions officers have told me that earlier is better than later.

Most policies will help you plan your homeschooling. For example, Stanford's admission information letter to homeschooled applicants says: "...we do not have a required curriculum or set of courses for applicants to Stanford. . . primarily we want them [applicants] to be able to demonstrate that they have successfully undertaken a serious, rigorous course of study. They should definitely provide a detailed description of their curriculum when they apply, but it is not necessary to follow a prescribed or approved homeschooling program... the central issue for us is how they have gone about the learning process, not how many hurdles they have jumped."

What does this tell you? Several things, I think. First, students planning to apply to Stanford need not enroll in an accredited independent-study program to generate an official record. A detailed home-brew transcript (as described in Chapter V) will do the trick. Second, studying, say, biology with several in-depth projects will probably work at least as well as a standard textbook biology course. Third, omitting something like foreign language does not automatically relegate an application to the reject pile.

Wheaton College, a selective, conservative Christian school in Illinois, sends out a complete packet for homeschooled applicants. Call their admissions office to obtain one free. The packet includes a suggested high school curriculum, a reading list, and a home schooling questionnaire. If your student plans to apply to Wheaton, they have made it very easy to "plan high school."

Unfortunately, some colleges and universities, as of this writing (late 1999), have highly discriminatory policies. Probably the most glaring examples are the Georgia state colleges, including institutions like Georgia Institute of Technology. Their policies require up to eight (the number increases each year) SAT II (Achievement Tests) of homeschoolers, but none of other applicants. Worse yet, homeschooled applicants need to score at least 650 out of 800—a very high score—on these tests. Finally, any homeschooler accepted needs to qualify in the top 40% of the admitted class. No squeaking in!

What to do about these policies? You have several options. First, vote with your feet. Look elsewhere. Second, work with your local and state homeschooling organizations to have these policies changed. Third, if a state school is responsible for these policies, let your state legislators know of your displeasure. Fourth, if your student is truly outstanding in some other way (published writer, Westinghouse Science Winner, National Merit Scholarship Finalist), try applying anyway, and see what happens.

Our Secret Weapon

Homeschoolers applying to college have an another edge.

Before and during the admissions process, the homeschooling family has full responsibility for researching schools, registering and preparing for standardized tests, completing applications, and preparing a transcript or portfolio. Working without the assistance of high school counselors may seem like a handicap. Just the opposite is true, however.

Instead, students attending public and private school are at a disadvantage. They and their parents assume someone else, usually a school counselor, is handling many of these tasks. At most high schools, however, administrators and counselors treat college applications in a cursory way. Little thought and no oversight go into the process. Researching colleges often consists of a counselor making a few offhand suggestions. All too often, non-homeschooled students miss or fail to completely document outside activities.

In contrast, homeschool families know that research and documentation is their responsibility. They are not in a position to delegate. Homeschooling parents, intimately familiar with their children, generally do a much more comprehensive job than public schools. Their thorough research leads to painstaking, clearly presented documentation. Homeschooled applicants and their parents compile impressive presentations.

Do-It-Yourself Works

Family-generated documents are all that you need for your homeschooler's college applications. Some homeschoolers are more comfortable using transcripts from outside sources like independent-study schools. By relying completely on an external transcript, however, homeschoolers run the same risk as students attending school. External transcripts seldom include all educational experiences.

Elite colleges and universities have accepted thousands of home-schooled students with their home-brew transcripts, portfolios, and diplomas. When it comes to homeschooling, high school accreditation does not matter to college admissions officers. What counts is the quality of the documentation. Is it thorough and complete? Does it accurately depict the student's abilities and accomplishments?

Homeschooling parents should think of themselves as the administrators of a small private school. Homeschooling is legal in all fifty states, and parents are undeniably performing administrative functions. As private school administrators, parents put together transcript or portfolio information and decide how to grant credits and grades (Chapter V).

Because homeschoolers succeed in college admissions with a variety of formats, there is no one best way to apply to college. Some students submit portfolios and letters of recommendation. As recounted in *College Admissions: A Guide For Homeschoolers* (now out of print but available through used book dealers), author Judy Gelner's son Kendall, without a transcript or diploma, was admitted to Rice University and offered a substantial scholarship. How? They put together an impressive portfolio.

Diverse transcript formats work. Some home-brew transcripts include grades and credits. Some show credits but no grades. Others simply list courses. The transcript may or may not contain course descriptions.

Similarly, homeschooling families generate their own diplomas, either by making up a form or by completing a pre-published blank form. A few colleges and universities do require General Education Development (GED) test results from graduates of non-accredited programs (most homeschoolers fall into this category). Usually these colleges will admit such students contingent on receiving a passing GED score. See Chapter IX for more information on the GED.

In short, you, the homeschooling family, can write your own portfolios or transcripts for college applications. You and the student are in the best position to document academic and extracurricular activities. Do-it-yourself not only works, but many find it preferable to relying completely on externally generated paperwork.

Chapter Highlights

- It is a buyer's market. Getting into most colleges is relatively easy.

- Alternatives to traditional college admissions include backdoor college admission, AP and CLEP testing, and college at home.

- Homeschoolers' eye-catching activities and projects can result in successful applications to selective schools.

- Admissions officers say that putting together a well-rounded student body takes precedence over recruiting well-rounded students.

- College admissions policies—where they exist—can help homeschoolers plan their high school homeschooling.

- Creating your own transcripts or portfolios works just as well as using an externally generated transcript.

And What About College?

CHAPTER III

HOME-BASED HIGH SCHOOL

Are you an experienced homeschooling parent, confident in your methods and able to clearly articulate your educational philosophy? If so, skip this chapter. Here, I plan to digress a bit from the main point of this book—college admissions for homeschoolers—and discuss different approaches to home education.

This detour grows out of my workshop, "High School Transcripts and College Applications," which I have presented to thousands of homeschooling families. My experience indicates that, without this information, I will spend the entire question and answer period fielding questions about how people homeschool, especially how they educate teenagers in home-based programs. This information applies to new homeschooling families as well as to those considering different approaches.

The second reason for this digression? As described in later chapters, college admissions officers will ask you and your teenager questions about your approach to home education and your educational philosophy. How do you homeschool and why have you chosen that approach? At the very least, I hope this chapter provides a few useful phrases for those situations.

If I were to interview one hundred homeschooling families with teenagers, I would hear one hundred different versions of high school at home. Homeschooling is idiosyncratic. It varies according to the family's educational philosophy and resources and the student's interests and goals.

Although families implement their ideas in myriad ways, in practice most home schools fall into one of four categories:

• Traditional/School-At-Home

• Unit-study Approach

• Interest-Initiated Learning/Unschooling

• Eclectic Education

Homeschoolers succeed with all of these methods at the high school level. And each approach has resulted in admissions to selective colleges.

The Traditional Approach

The traditional approach, also called school-at-home, is just what it sounds like. It is structured, with lesson plans, textbooks, quizzes and tests, subject-specific projects, and grades. The subjects closely parallel those taught at government schools. Usually the program includes English, science, math, and social studies (history or geography). Electives (optional courses) correspond to those of government and private schools: music, art, religious studies, physical education, and foreign language. The student may study every subject every day, just as he would at most high schools. Or his schedule may resemble college, with larger blocks of time devoted to individual subjects two or three days a week.

Students following a traditional approach also participate in extracurricular activities. Examples are 4-H, sports, music lessons, church youth groups, and volunteer work. While parents using traditional materials consider these activities vital, these families have decided to emphasize textbook learning. "Yes, you can go to your martial arts class if you have completed your math."

The educational philosophy behind the traditional approach is, "I-teach: you learn." The parent or program decides what is best for the teenager, and he covers the assigned material.

The principal advantage of the traditional approach is that parents know the drill. Most likely, they attended school and were taught this way. Generally, the student works out of a textbook, reading, doing problems, and answering questions. Every so often, he takes a test or writes a paper or does a major project related to the studies. A parent or an outside school evaluates the work and assigns grades. Some parents find comfort in the familiar sequence: read and write, test, grade.

Many parents use a school-at-home approach because they like knowing that, in their words, "All the bases are covered. Our teenager is learning what he is supposed to learn." Some families say their traditional methods work well for children who like school-type structure. Students motivated by grades, probably 10% or less, enjoy school-at-home.

At the high school level, teenagers often teach themselves using traditional-approach resources, that is, self-instructional books and study guides. This relieves parents of the necessity of re-learning geometry or biology—unless they want to!

Many experienced homeschoolers have discovered problems with the traditional approach. There are drawbacks. First, school-at-home can be the most expensive way to homeschool. Costs for textbooks alone may exceed several hundred dollars for a single year.

Also, school-at-home can be tedious and boring. Government schools prove this on a daily basis. This creates burnout. Often, I meet parents who feel overwhelmed by their teenager's homeschooling. They complain about too many hours devoted to curriculum each day and say, "I have to push him to do everything." When I question these parents closely, I almost always learn that they use an exclusively traditional approach.

Another disadvantage of school-at-home? Teenagers who did not like typical schoolwork are unlikely to do well when confronted with the same thing at home. These teens equate textbooks, texts, and grades with failure. Avoid traditional instructional materials with children who say, "If it looks like school, I can't do it." Try other approaches that provide hands-on, real world experiences.

In some cases, the traditional approach leads to over-dependence on teachers and programmed instructional materials. Students learn how to play the game, but they never learn how to learn or how to take advantage of community resources. Additionally, families may spend so much time "covering the material" that the student has no time to develop talents and to pursue interests.

What are your choices if you decide to conduct your high school homeschooling this way? One option involves enrolling the teenager in an independent study, correspondence high school (Appendix J). Just as in a public high school, students take core or required courses plus electives. The school mails materials (usually texts, tests, perhaps some laboratory equipment), and students submit work for grading at reasonable intervals. Prices range from as little as $150 per year up to more than $1,000 annually. Independent study schools issue transcripts and grant diplomas.

Alternatively, students may enroll in umbrella or satellite schools, private schools that help families homeschool. Umbrella schools may have local, statewide, or national enrollment. Some are very flexible with respect to methods and materials. Others are more structured, not unlike the independent study correspondence high schools described above. Umbrella and satellite schools prescribe record keeping and assist with course planning. With those records you complete, they generate a transcript and grant a diploma.

Many homeschoolers decide to bypass outside agencies and plan their own traditional curriculum. Using guidelines similar to those discussed in the next chapter, families design courses, purchase textbooks, give tests, and assign grades. In devising school-at-home, families have maximum flexibility in selection of materials, in scheduling, and in grading. They keep their own records, write their own transcripts and portfolios, and grant their own diplomas.

Unit Studies

A second approach to home education, using unit studies, is very popular with homeschooling families. To do a unit study, the student investigates a topic in depth. The topic may be academic or non-academic. Examples are: "Astronomy," "Japan," "Classic Film," "Nutrition," and "Horses." In exploring the topic, the student eventually covers most school subjects (math, science, social studies, language arts).

As an example, let's say a student is interested in birds. He might plan the following learning activities:

- Read and write about birds and famous ornithologists (Language Arts, Science)

- Diagram and outline life cycles, habitats, ecology of birds (Science, Math)

- Reconstruct a chicken skeleton (Science)

- Study the aerodynamics of flight (Math, Science)

- Diagram the migration pathways of birds (Geography)

- Sketch birds (Art)

- Cook birds (Home Economics)

Unit studies are more open-ended than school-at-home. Teenagers work on units for a day or a week or a year. Unit studies prompt more interaction with the real world and involve hands-on projects more often than school-at-home. Generally, students pursuing unit studies will use real books and real world resources (libraries, people, computers, and so on) rather than textbooks.

From the standpoint of educational philosophy, kids doing unit studies work from real world specifics to general concepts. They learn the Pythagorean theorem from squaring up a building project. They study biology in the context of caring for horses. The word "discovery" applies here. Instead of being told what to learn, unit studies encourage teenagers to draw their own conclusions.

Like their counterparts using traditional materials, students building their homeschooling around thematic units will also engage in a wide range of outside activities. Sometimes it will be possible to make these activities part of a unit. As an example, volunteering in a veterinary clinic might be a portion of a zoology unit.

Many home educators prefer unit studies because thematic units seem to encourage more curiosity and independent thinking than traditional materials. Most students find unit studies more involving and entertaining than a steady diet of texts and tests. Units, by definition, are interdisciplinary, crossing over school subject lines, just like in the real world. Some teenagers say that they retain more with this format.

Unit studies often motivate children to go beyond the planned unit. In the process, the student becomes an independent learner. This clearly provides an advantage for a high school student wishing to pursue a topic in which the parents have no expertise or interest.

Of course, unit studies are not for everyone. They do not work well in families where parents have no patience with the discovery approach to education. It is harder to know if students are learning, in the words of some homeschooling parents, "what they should." Unit studies can require the frequent use of outside resources—like the library—and may not be a good choice for those with limited time or transportation.

Homeschooling families can purchase pre-planned unit studies from several sources (Appendix J). Guides to help plan your own units are also available. Some umbrella schools and satellite schools (for example, Clonlara) will give high school credit to those using the unit study format. Creating your own transcript or portfolio based on thematic units (see Chapter V) is another option.

Unschooling or Interest-Initiated Learning

Unschooling or interest-initiated learning is a third approach to homeschooling. Students in unschooling environments select and direct their own projects and activities. Unschooling parents help their teenagers pursue their interests rather than the subjects listed on a suggested course of study.

The unschooled student may spend weeks or months with computers or art projects or even auto repair. The conscientious unschooling parent functions as a facilitator, supporting the student by planning collaboratively, helping with expenses, and searching for resources. Most unschooling families only buy curriculum if the student has determined that using traditional materials will help him reach his goal.

Teenage unschoolers often participate in community activities. They volunteer at the library, spend time with local drama groups, work at hospitals, and stuff envelopes for political campaigns. Many hold paying positions in various settings.

In unschooling families, student-selected activities and real life comprise the core of the curriculum. Running a small business is consumer math and bookkeeping and language arts. Gardening is science. Reading the newspaper is social studies. Planning and preparing dinner is home economics. Often students and parents determine curriculum after the fact.

In unschooling households, parents translate interest-initiated learning into educationese, the language of high school course descriptions, to create transcripts. This process will be described more fully in Chapter V.

Clearly, the educational philosophy behind unschooling differs from the traditional and unit-study approaches. "Students learn best when their interests direct the learning," probably sums it up best.

Advantages of unschooling are many. With community activities and everyday life at the core, interest-initiated learning can be inexpensive. Unschooling is flexible and hands-on, a boon for school-phobic students. Most importantly, because unschoolers assume responsibility for their education, they, the students, often become self-directed learners. Interest-initiated learning works well for teenagers with a deep abiding interest or hobby as well as for students with clearly delineated goals.

You have probably already thought of the primary drawback of unschooling—it does not look like school. This makes parents nervous, relatives nervous, neighbors nervous. Most parents have to read a great deal about interest-initiated learning to overcome their previous conditioning. They restructure their thinking to realize the advantages of unschooling. For those without previous homeschooling experience, this can be a tall order.

Other drawbacks? Some say that unschooling results in educational gaps, holes in a student's knowledge. Teens who spend hours each day programming computers, for example, may not find time to read Shakespeare. There is a trade-off. Unschooling families have decided, up front, that self-direction is more important than imparting a broad, arbitrarily selected spectrum of knowledge.

So, interest-initiated learning does not look like school, and it may contain holes. Yet many unschoolers have become computer wizards, successful business operators, published writers, inventors, and so on. This makes them very attractive to selective colleges. Issues of *Growing Without Schooling*, the bimonthly magazine devoted to unschooling, recount numerous instances of selective colleges and universities admitting unschoolers.

Preparation for unschooling, as indicated above, requires that parents thoroughly immerse themselves in reading about interest-initiated learning. See Appendix J for suggested resources. Highly recommended reading for students and parents is Grace Llewellyn's *The Teenage Liberation Handbook*.

Help is available for those families who want to unschool. Several umbrella and satellite schools convert unschooling activities into transcripts (Clonlara for example). Alternatively, as with other approaches, the family need not involve themselves with an outside agency. Parents have the option of writing the transcript and granting a diploma according to the guidelines in Chapter V.

The Eclectic Approach

A fourth method of homeschooling, the eclectic approach, combines traditional materials, unit studies, unschooling time, and anything else that works. Families incorporate diverse resources to create the best program for the student. The educational philosophy is: use anything that encourages enthusiasm for learning. Work collaboratively with the student. Change methods and resources when the student seems to be losing interest. Appendix E includes sample eclectic curricula.

The eclectic approach emphasizes flexibility to tailor educational experiences to the student, without an overlay of educational philosophy. Parents respond to changing student needs in an ad-hoc fashion. Students, especially teens, are given a lot of freedom. Without the philosophical constraints of unschooling, parents also feel free to impose subjects they deem essential.

With the eclectic approach, a balance exists between the traditional and the innovative, a balance with which most parents and students are comfortable. Students not only learn how to learn—due mostly to the unschooling component of this approach—they also learn how to handle traditional materials and in-depth projects or unit studies. Together with their parents, students discover how to locate educational resources in the community and how to evaluate those resources.

Our son and daughter enrolled in a diploma-granting, independent study program. Still we considered ourselves eclectic home educators. Why? Both Jeff and Tamara, in completing 16 units with American School, worked with traditional materials one to two hours daily. They devoted the most of each day to activities they planned: flying practice, reading, art, music, hiking, volunteer work, and other pursuits.

The primary disadvantage of the eclectic approach is that parents may lack the confidence to work cooperatively with their teenagers to put together such a program. Additionally, the constant communication between parent and student and the resulting readjustment of studies and activities makes some families uncomfortable.

The eclectic approach, like the school-at-home, unit studies, and unschooling, can be independently implemented by the homeschooling family. In this case, of course, the family will generate the transcript and issue the diploma. As an alternative, the student enrolls in a diploma-granting umbrella school that does not specify a set curriculum.

Which Approach?

All these methods are effective. And, in practice, most homeschooling families do not fit exactly into one of four neat categories. Linda Dobson, in *Homeschooling: The Early Years*, points instead to a continuum of homeschooling practice, from structured and traditional to unstructured and child-led. In addition, families often switch gears. As needed, they adopt different approaches to get the job done.

Why specify four approaches then? These categories can help you articulate what you do and why you do it. You will need information about pros and cons of different approaches in the application process. An overview of the four categories also begins to illustrate the wide range of successful homeschooling practice for those new to the idea of home education.

With respect to college entrance, does it matter which of the above methods of homeschooling your family adopts? Probably not. Homeschooled teens from a wide variety of educational backgrounds have been admitted to selective institutions nationwide. Record keeping and transcripts, as described in Chapter V, will work with any of the methods. Documentation is the key.

In deciding among overall approaches and in selecting materials, you will make mistakes. As my father is fond of saying, "The only people who don't make mistakes are those who don't do anything." Remember, compared to government schools, you have an edge. When you detect a mistake, you can fix it. You do not have to wait for a new teacher or until the end of the school year.

Remember, by deciding how to homeschool, you have home-grown expertise right in front of your nose. Ask your student what he thinks about various options and programs and resources. You may have to ask more than once, but I guarantee that eventually most teenagers will tell you. Involve the student in the process.

Proceed with what best fits your situation. How can families ultimately decide what fits? Try the following check list:

- Know and understand your options.

- Educate yourself about resources.

- Discuss student's goals and priorities.

- Discuss parents' goals and priorities.

- Think of your own formal and informal educational experiences; describe what you believe about how people learn best.

- Rely on your sense of what "feels right" for your family.

Chapter Highlights

Descriptions of four major approaches to homeschooling—traditional, unit study, unschooling, and eclectic—help parents and students describe what they do and why they do it, in other words, define educational philosophy.

There is no One Best Approach. Unschoolers and eclectic homeschoolers win college admission just as often as teenagers using thematic units and traditional programs.

CHAPTER IV

GUIDELINES FOR HIGH SCHOOL AND COLLEGE PREPARATORY WORK

You have done it—made the decision to homeschool through high school. Or you have just begun homeschooling your teen. After debating the pros and cons of various homeschooling approaches, you decide exactly what to include. With college right around the corner, many say, "I want to get it just right. I do not want to jeopardize my student's chances of being admitted to his first-choice college."

Whether you put together your own materials or select an independent study course, you will need criteria for evaluating resources and programs. What guidelines are available? Is it more important to mimic local high schools or pay attention to college requirements? How does preparation for the principal college admissions tests, SAT II and ACT, figure into a high school program? How do homeschooling families accomplish program planning without the assistance of a high school counselor?

Scope and Sequence

Homeschoolers often turn to a scope and sequence to determine what to cover. "Scope and sequence" is a little bit of educationese that need not frighten you. Scope equals what, and sequence equals when. A scope and sequence describes who learns what when. Teachers, state education departments, university professors, and textbook publishers all write scope and sequences. "You mean to tell me," some homeschooling parents ask, "that no one definitive scope and sequence exists?" That's right.

Scope and sequence or suggested course of study information is widely available. Often local school districts will supply their version. *World Book Encyclopedia* distributes one free for grades kindergarten through twelve. Many homeschool publishers, like A Beka Books and Bob Jones University Press, also provide free scope and sequences. William Bennett's James Madison High School is a particularly well thought-out traditional scope and sequence (see Cathy Duffy's *Christian Home Educators' Curriculum Manual, Junior/Senior High*).

Scope and sequences make interesting reading, especially if you have time to review several. As you peruse suggested courses of study from different sources, you will notice a disconcerting variability summed up best by saying that they do not match.

First, different authors recommend different courses for each grade. Second, some scope and sequences list subjects that others ignore entirely. For example the *World Book Encyclopedia* scope and sequence lists world geography and advanced map skills as part of a ninth grade curriculum. A Beka Books says nothing about map skills or geography under ninth grade, but includes units on the American free enterprise system and on liberal versus conservative thought.

Too often, in reviewing scope and sequence information, families worry unnecessarily about doing everything. They want to cross all the T's and dot all the I's on a given course listing. What a waste of time. Homeschooling parents who have reviewed several courses of study realize that no one item is critical. Items that are making them crazy, subjects their teenager simply will not do, are omitted on alternate, equally valid or invalid course listings.

Any scope and sequence reflects the author's educational philosophy and worldview. Authors may build a suggested course of study around anything—from conservative Christianity to modern political correctness. If you use scope and sequences, do so only after reading several to find one compatible with your views (see Appendix J).

Some homeschoolers use scope and sequences not as curriculum imperatives, but instead as sources of ideas. One family uses the reading lists from a high school English course of study when looking for new authors to sample. Another family follows the suggested math program of a local high school.

Other homeschooling parents argue that following a scope and sequence ensures broad coverage of typical high school subject material. They look for well-written courses of study that avoid repeating the same material from grade to grade. Using a single course of study creates a consistent approach and worldview. Families who do not know where to begin appreciate the structure of a course of study, once they have reviewed several.

In our experience, scope and sequences are helpful only as general guides. All homeschooling families should think carefully about going beyond typical courses of study information. A scope and sequence only answers the question: what does this scope and sequence author deem important? I suggest, instead, that you address three different questions to determine what to cover.

- What are the student's abilities, talents, and goals?

- What do you think is important?

- What are colleges seeking?

College Requirements

What do colleges want? Mostly they want capable students who can complete their programs. Selective colleges and universities look also for intellectual spark, in other words students who demonstrate a thirst for learning.

More specifically, colleges and universities evaluate several pieces of evidence to help them rank applicants. This evidence includes courses taken, grade point average, standardized test scores, essays, extracurricular activities, interviews, recommendations, and awards.

Schools list suggested courses of study in their catalogs and "view books," which are basically free sales-pitch brochures. The courses of study differ according to the competitiveness of the college or university. Several suggested high school courses, taken from Barron's *Profiles of American Colleges,* are listed below.

Williams College (Massachusetts)
Barron's Ranking: Most Competitive
  English—4 years
  Math—4 years
  Foreign Language—3-4 years
  Science—2-3 years
  Social Studies—2-3 years

Trinity University (Texas)
Barron's Ranking: Highly Competitive
  English— 4 years
  Math—3-4 years
  Foreign Language—2-3 years
  Science—2-3 years
  Social Studies—2-3 years

University of Oregon (Oregon)
Barron's Ranking: Very Competitive
  English—4 years
  Math—3 years
  Social Studies—3 years
  Science—2 years
  Foreign Language—2 years

So, you might well assume the obvious. Colleges want exactly what they say they want—documentation of certain courses. To achieve this, homeschoolers may devise their own studies, or they may purchase courses from independent study high schools. The less obvious? College admissions officers often find alternatives not only acceptable but also preferable. Alternatives that demonstrate the student far exceeds typical high school standards are in demand. Examples would be an in-depth science project, writing and publishing a book, or running a business.

Consider a homeschooler who studies reptiles to the point where he has earned the moniker, herpetologist. He has published several papers and presented one at a nationwide conference. This same teenager also completed a home-study chemistry course, but no other science. And he never got around to studying a foreign language. Is he out of luck with selective colleges?

Not at all. Assuming decent standardized test scores, the herpetology activities will be so impressive that admissions officers will be eager to accept him, regardless of his formal course work. They will probably give him a waiver for the foreign language or simply require that he take it at college.

Consider another example. An advanced piano student impresses the audition committee of a selective music school. They will not care that he never took a foreign language or that geometry was his most advanced math course.

The Homeschooling Advantage

Ignoring your teenager's interests and goals by exclusively following a suggested course of study may create a pretty transcript. Like all well-rounded students, she can prove geometry theorems, name state capitals, balance chemical reactions, and recite early American poetry. Conventional wisdom says that this is exactly what colleges want.

However, in practice it seems that a nice paper trail is just that. The well-rounded teen risks being lost in the crowd of applicants with similar documentation. These well-rounded, but otherwise unremarkable students do not necessarily come out on top when competing for scholarships and slots at selective colleges.

To avoid this scenario, we planned our homeschooling backwards.

Many home educators prioritize high school academics and fill in student-directed activities around them. We adopted precisely the opposite approach. In setting up our high school programs, we prioritized Jeff's and Tamara's activities—those things they would do without our urging—and filled in academics around the activities.

Our first task every semester consisted of listing the student's current activities. We also discussed talents and short-term and long-term goals. Next we brainstormed ideas for capitalizing on the talents and goals and added these to the current activities list. Finally, I translated the list into educationese, the language of high school course descriptions.

In compiling our lists, we often discovered that our teenagers were already covering many school subjects. For example, Jeff was editor of Civil Air Patrol newsletter (Language Arts). Tamara spent hours and hours reading historical fiction (Contemporary Literature and History) and writing stories (English). Both children hiked in the mountains at every opportunity (Physical Education) and played piano an hour each day (Fine Arts).

After deciding how much school the kids' activities covered, we would refer back to college entrance requirements to fill in gaps. Both Jeff and Tamara wanted to apply to selective colleges, most of which list advanced math and foreign language in their suggested courses of study. Student-selected activities did not adequately cover these subjects, so we usually bought math and foreign language programs.

Should you build your curriculum around college entrance requirements? If your teenager will apply to college, yes. You could pattern your homeschooling after high school graduation requirements, but that simply creates an unnecessary filter. Contact colleges of interest, not high schools, and work with their suggested preparation. Look for ways to exceed those requirements in areas where your teens excel. If your child loves languages, do Latin and French and German. Do not restrict her to a single language, fearful that she will never have time to cover all of world history. Students' strengths get admissions officers' attention and create a warm, supportive educational environment at home. To paraphrase one on-line bulletin board contributor, "We bought courses for our daughter's weaknesses, but now that she's in college, I wish we had spent more money on her passions." Focus on the donut, not the hole.

Finally, educate your student to your specifications. The question "What do we have to do?" results in frustrating sessions with uncompleted checklists. Instead consider, "What can we do? What excites this teenager?" Do not restrict yourself to government high school requirements or colleges' recommended courses. Build on your teenagers' strengths, and homeschooling achievements may exceed those of any suggested list of high school courses. As a homeschooling family, you have the flexibility and the time to do it right. Take advantage of it.

College Admissions Testing

A final curricular consideration concerns preparation for standardized tests. Most important are the Preliminary Scholastic Assessment Test (PSAT), the Scholastic Assessment Test I (SAT I, previously called the Scholastic Aptitude Test), and the test administered by the American College Testing Program (ACT).

The top selective institutions also require results of one or more one-hour SAT II Subject Tests (formerly called Achievement Tests), which cover areas like English Literature, Math, Chemistry, and Spanish. Lastly, some colleges and universities give admissions preference and college credit for good Advanced Placement (AP) test results.

What are these tests? The Preliminary Scholastic Assessment Test, although optional, serves two purposes. First and foremost, a stellar performance may result in a National Merit Scholarship, hence the alternative name of the PSAT—the National Merit Scholarship Qualifying Test, NMSQT. Second, taking the PSAT gives students a chance to take an SAT-like test prior to taking the required test, the SAT I.

Students may take the PSAT as sophomores and juniors, but only the score attained in the next-to-last year, usually the junior year of high school, counts towards qualifying for National Merit Scholarships. This need not concern home educators much except to note that some homeschooled students complete high school one or more years early. If you anticipate this happening, be careful which school year you list on the PSAT registration materials.

Unlike other tests for which individuals register by mail or telephone, students must register for the PSAT with public and private schools. An occasional umbrella or satellite school may make PSAT testing available to students. Generally, though, you will have to work through the counselors of a local high school to register your teenager for the test.

Home educators should know about one additional, minor complication to the PSAT. The test is given only once each year, in October. Students sign up for the test several weeks in advance. Contact local high schools in late August and early September to ensure that you do not miss registration deadlines. Some parents recommend making preliminary arrangements in May, before summer vacation.

Content of the PSAT changed in 1997. The test now consists of three parts: verbal, math, and writing skills. The three parts are added together to create a "Selection Index" for National Merit Scholarships. Thus, the scholarship program favors students with impressive verbal abilities over mathematical wizards. Do not be overly concerned about this. Less than one percent of teenagers nationwide qualify for National Merit Scholarships. Most obtain college funding from other sources.

The tests of primary interest are the Scholastic Assessment Test, also called the Reasoning Test or the SAT I, and the test of the American College Testing Program (ACT). Many colleges use either an SAT I or an ACT score to rank students with other applicants.

Some admissions officers say that these test results give them independent, unbiased evaluations of homeschoolers. For that reason, test scores mean more for homeschooled applicants than they do for students applying from regular high schools. That is the bad news.

The good news? An increasing number of colleges and universities are making SAT and ACT scores optional for admissions to bachelor degree programs. They agree with the disclaimer at the College Board Web site: "The SAT I does not measure motivation, creativity, or special talents (even though these qualities will contribute to your success in college and throughout life)." For a list of the almost 300 schools nationwide who no longer use SAT or ACT scores to admit students, write to FairTest or visit their website. See Appendix J for contact information.

The current SAT I includes verbal and math sections. The literature accompanying the test registration materials says that the test measures reasoning abilities rather than specific subject content. For example, examinees interpret scientific data in a reading passage rather than recall specific scientific principles.

In 1996, the College Board, who brings you all these tests, recentered the SAT. An average (50th percentile) SAT score is now 1000 (500 on the verbal portion, 500 on the math); previously, the average score hovered in the 900 range. Although no direct conversion exists to compare old scores to new scores, generally new, recentered scores are higher than old scores. According to Michele Hernandez in *A Is For Admission*, in Ivy League admissions offices a 1400 SAT used to be considered an excellent score; now that number is 1500.

The ACT focuses on content to a greater extent than the SAT, which means the ACT is more likely to include recall-type test items. ACT literature states that the test measures knowledge, understanding, and skills acquired throughout the student's education. ACT sections include English, Math, Reading, and Science Reasoning.

Both tests are given at locations worldwide several times each year. High school students, homeschoolers included, typically take these tests either the spring of their junior year or the fall of their senior year. Students register online or with materials obtained from any high school or directly from the SAT I and ACT administrators (Appendix J).

Most colleges require scores from one of these two tests. The SAT I is more common on the East and West Coasts, the ACT in the Midwest. To determine which test a given school requires, find the college's Internet site or see Barron's *Profiles of American Colleges* and other college guides at your library. Sometimes schools will take either test result. In that case, you may want to have your teens prepare for both. They can then take the test with which they feel most comfortable.

Include test preparation in your high school curriculum. This is extremely important. Familiarity with the test format and experience working in a timed situation can increase a student's score.

How to prepare? Obtain free practice materials from the counseling office of the nearest high school or directly from the SAT I and ACT publishers. Both the SAT I and the ACT publishers distribute guides with test-taking tips, sample questions, and practice tests. New guides come out late each summer.

Additionally, there are many private companies that provide preparation materials for college admissions tests. Books available in the study guide section of large bookstores can help the student prepare at home. Some libraries also carry these study guides. Recently, several computer programs dealing with test preparation have appeared on the market. Appendix J includes test preparation book and computer program titles.

Conventional wisdom has held that beating these tests by using preparation guides or courses usually only increases scores by 100-150 points on the SAT. Homeschoolers should test that wisdom, however. One homeschooled teen I met in Florida said she and her mother did intensive SAT math preparation for a solid year. She raised her SAT math score from the low 400's to the mid 700's, out of a possible 800.

Of course, the best preparation for the SAT I and ACT is a well-rounded education. The debate over what constitutes a well-rounded education is complicated and never-ending. Nevertheless, certain people ace these tests. Those who read widely, write frequently, and learn math through geometry and two years of algebra excel.

Students will only need SAT II Subject (Achievement) Test scores if they apply to high-powered, selective schools. Examples are colleges like Harvard, UC Berkeley, Brandeis, and MIT. SAT II Subject (Achievement) Tests, demonstrate competency in specific areas like Math, Spanish, English Literature, and Biology.

Some homeschoolers whose test results have been mediocre in the past may want to consider taking one or more SAT II Subject Tests — even if the target college does not require it. Why? Unlike the SAT I, you can actually study specific content and do well on the SAT II tests. Preparation time for an SAT II Subject Test will more likely result in a higher score than preparation time devoted to the SAT I.

Selective colleges and universities usually require one to three SAT II Subject Tests, the Writing Test being most frequently requested. Most large bookstores carry study guides for these tests. The SAT publishers also provide a study guide and sample test with the registration materials.

Advanced Placement (AP) tests are unique. Some colleges use the scores to give the student college credit for work done in high school. Good AP test scores also enhance college applications by showing that the student went above and beyond typical high school level work. Colleges offer advanced placement in more than twenty high school subjects, including French, Math, Physics, World History, and so on.

Obtain study guides from the AP test publishers and at large bookstores. Use these guides to ascertain if your teenagers' preparation will allow him do well on these tests. The guides can also help you plan a course of study that will lead to a passing score.

To sum up, for most students, preparation for the PSAT and SAT or ACT will be sufficient. Teenagers competing for places at selective colleges as well as homeschoolers who test poorly on general standardized tests like the SAT I, should also prepare for one to three SAT II Subject Tests and possibly one or more Advanced Placement examinations.

Begin preparation for these tests in grade eight or nine. This may sound early. Factor in, though, that many homeschooled students complete high school ahead of schedule. Homeschoolers are not smarter than everyone else, but homeschooling itself is very efficient! Consider, also, that your teen may take the PSAT as early as grade ten. Beginning preparation in grade eight or nine is right on target.

There are several methods of preparing for the tests. Our teenagers took practice test sections once monthly. We would then score and discuss the results. Study guides are also helpful. We particularly liked The Princeton Review's *Cracking The New SAT and PSAT.*

In discussing high school with home educators nationwide, I have come to the conclusion that successful programs emerge and unfold. They evolve. And they have to start somewhere, so planning is important. As a friend of mine, a mother who homeschooled four children through high school, says, "Failure to plan is planning to fail."

Just as important, however, is the family's response to the changing needs of teenagers. Factor it all in: scope and sequence, college requirements, students' interests and goals, and admissions testing. Finally, listen to your apprentice-adults, your teenagers, and individualize your program to make the most of these years.

Chapter Highlights

- Homeschoolers use scope and sequences—lists of who learns what when—as general guidelines, as sources of ideas, and as curriculum outlines. No one scope and sequence or course of study covers everything.

- College requirements vary in accordance with selectivity.

- Homeschoolers have the time and flexibility to exceed college entrance requirements in their areas of expertise.

- College applicants can ignore standardized tests by applying to colleges where such tests are optional.

- PSAT, SAT I, SAT II, and ACT preparation materials are widely available. Begin preparation in grade 8 or 9.

- Scope and sequence information, the student's talents and interests, college admissions requirements, and preparation for college admissions tests—account for them all in planning high school.

And What About College?

CHAPTER V

RECORD KEEPING AND TRANSCRIPTS

It is winter, 1992. I am staring at a big folder labeled "Jeff." The folder contains work samples, award certificates, programs, test scores, Civil Air Patrol newsletters, notices from the diving team, church bulletins, community college course descriptions, and more.

Those folder contents comprise all of one and one-half years of record keeping for Jeff's home-based high school program. Jeff needs this data converted to an intelligible format for an application to "The Making Of An Engineer," a summer college-credit program for high school students at the University of Denver. Specifically, the application requests a transcript.

I toyed with the idea of doing a portfolio. The thought, "Let them add it up and figure it out," had some appeal. I knew homeschoolers had been successful using portfolios to gain admission to selective colleges (*College Admissions: A Guide For Homeschoolers* by Judy Gelner). However, arguments for writing a transcript were strong, at least in Jeff's case.

Jeff had credit from an independent study high school and from two colleges. He also had spent a lot of time on his interests, electronics and flying, and on community activities like Civil Air Patrol and volunteer work. We wanted admissions officers to understand all of Jeff's preparation, not only the academic parts.

Combining all academic with less traditional learning activities into a master transcript allowed us to present consistent, integrated, easy-to-understand data. Jeff would be applying to very traditional colleges and programs. In line with their educational philosophy, we felt that writing a transcript rather than compiling a portfolio made more sense, especially since some of the courses were non-traditional. For more details, search libraries and used bookstores for the out-of-print book, *College Admissions: A Guide for Homeschoolers* by Judy Gelner.

Finally, even though aspects of our homeschooling were non-traditional, I preferred writing a transcript to compiling a portfolio. What can I say? It is just a personal preference. I like numbers and columns, and so does Jeff.

Transcripts Versus Portfolios

Selective colleges need written proof—documentation—of educational achievements, of homeschooling. The documentation allows admissions officers to rank students with other applicants and determine if a student will do well at their school. Documentation includes portfolios, transcripts, standardized test scores, letters of recommendation, student essays, interview reports, and other data. Two types of family-generated documentation commonly accompany college applications from homeschooled students: a portfolio or a transcript.

A portfolio consists of descriptions and examples of the student's work and accomplishments. In addition to work samples, it may include programs, articles, photos, letters of recommendation, and more. Usually the student or parents also write a letter describing the homeschooling program.

Homeschoolers submit portfolios, together with the standardized test scores and basic application information (name, address, birth date, and other data required for all applications), instead of transcripts. For more details, read one family's successful experience with this approach (*College Admissions: A Guide For Homeschoolers* by Judy Gelner).

With the portfolio approach, you ask the school to understand and evaluate your teenager on your terms. The portfolio acts as a screening device. Portfolio advocates explain, "If they cannot handle a portfolio, this college is not the right place for our student." Admissions officers reviewing portfolios look for evidence of superior achievement in one or more areas. They will not necessarily try to fit the student's accomplishments into their list of suggested high school studies.

Portfolio submissions appear risky. However, some students will do better with a portfolio than a transcript. A portfolio may best represent and depict the activities of some unschoolers—those whose homeschooling is based on student-directed projects and on real world experiences. The unschooler who has pursued one or more interests in depth should have little trouble making a good presentation.

In some cases a transcript magnifies weaknesses and obscures strengths. A teenager who runs a business can put his experience into transcript format, but his background will be more impressive as a portfolio presentation. An award-winning artist or computer programmer who has successfully marketed his ideas may find himself in a similar position.

Some colleges and universities consider themselves highly innovative. They look for students with non-traditional backgrounds and non-traditional documentation. Examples are Antioch College in Ohio and Colorado College in Colorado (see Appendix G). A portfolio submission usually impresses admissions officers at these non-traditional schools.

Portfolios do present difficulties. Due to time constraints, some admissions officers have to do everything by the numbers. They use formulas incorporating grade point averages (GPA) and standardized test scores. Without a transcript and GPA, they cannot calculate an applicant ranking that says "admit" or "reject." This is particularly true at some large state colleges and universities. Portfolios can make the job of reviewing candidates so onerous that admissions officers at some large institutions will simply suggest that the student apply elsewhere.

Additionally, portfolios run the risk of being rejected by the occasional admissions officer who tries to fit portfolio data into the list of recommended college preparatory high school courses. Reports also indicate that junior college admissions personnel find portfolios baffling.

Advantages of Transcripts

The solution? Consider writing a home-brew master transcript. Put on your translator hat to convert documentation into a familiar format. List courses. Write course descriptions. Recount high school homeschooling on their terms. A transcript makes it easy for colleges to understand and categorize your student according to their criteria.

Homeschooled students who have used traditional and unit study materials, in whole or in part, will find a transcript readily documents their work. A transcript also documents unschooling activities and projects, more easily than you might guess.

The benefits of writing a master transcript are many. For students applying to a large state college or university, a transcript provides admissions personnel with the numbers they need. Community college applicants will spend less time explaining homeschooling. Conservative college admissions officers understand transcripts better than portfolios.

Furthermore, transcripts serve other purposes. Some insurance companies offer lower driver's insurance rates to students who maintain a "B" average. You can prove that your student has a "B" average with a transcript. Some states require transcripts to obtain student work permits, generally needed for legal paid employment of workers ages 13 to 15. A transcript can help your teenager win admission to special programs for high school students, programs like Aviation Challenge at Space Camp or Talent Search at various universities. Applications for scholarships not administered by college financial aid offices, like local awards and ROTC scholarships, often require transcripts.

Now that we have written several transcripts and updates, I have also been pleasantly surprised by how transcripts motivate teens. They see the finished product and realize just how much they have accomplished. Many students increase their efforts just to enhance the transcript!

As previously stated, writing a transcript does not commit the family to school-at-home. A transcript format works for all homeschooling approaches: unschoolers, those who use a unit study approach, traditionalists, and eclectics, like us.

Ideally, beginning in ninth grade, homeschoolers should update their transcripts semi-annually or annually. This readies your teen for all eventualities and takes advantage of the motivation some derive from the transcript. Finally, if you find yourself in the situation we faced with Jeff, your high school documentation may be sketchy. If so, put on the coffee, stay up late a few nights, and you can recover. We reconstructed what happened and wrote a transcript after the fact, and so can you. We detail the process later in this chapter.

Record Keeping

Prior to writing a transcript, homeschooling families need a database. This database includes records and documents that reflect the student's work and achievements. You may have other records. Correspondence and umbrella schools dictate certain record keeping. State statute or local regulations may also specify that you keep certain records.

Whatever your situation, you will find that record keeping makes it easier to write a transcript or compile a portfolio. It is worth your time. Having a well-organized transcript or portfolio simplifies the college application process.

Some homeschooled teenagers enroll in independent study institutions. In these cases, the school generates records, usually including a transcript. Do not rely completely on their record keeping, however. There are exceptions, but most umbrella and correspondence schools primarily record academic accomplishments. Often they only recognize subjects for which their school gives credit.

As an example, American School, an independent study high school, grants credit for French and Spanish, which they offer. They will not give credit for German or Latin, which they do not offer. Similarly, their school does not offer music or physical education, and they deny credit for these subjects. Even for students enrolled in independent study programs, homeschooling families should assume responsibility for documentation. Remember the goal—to give admissions officers a complete list of your teenager's accomplishments.

So, how do you do this? First, regardless of records kept elsewhere, create your own. An article by homeschooling parent Terri Endsley describes an easy, all-encompassing record keeping system (see Appendix K). To implement this system, all you need is a yearly calendar with big boxes for each day. Each morning, weekends included, your teen records his previous day. He or she lists both academic and non-academic activities. With each activity, they indicate the amount of time spent, rounded off to the nearest half-hour, and a school subject coding. Here are some examples from our kids' high school years.

From Jeff's Calendar:
 Monday, May 18
   Breakfast for family 1/2 IL
   Newspaper/morning news/discussion 1/2 SS
   Math 1-1/2 M
   Piano Practice 1 FA
   Bike ride 1 PE
   Am Hist 1 SS
   CAP Newsletter 2 LA
   Model Rocket 1 S
   Yard work 2 PE

From Tamara's Calendar:

Wednesday, April 3

Newspaper/morning news/discussion 1/2 SS

Anne of Green Gables 2 LA

Math 1 M

Geography Game 1 SS

4-H Sewing 2 IL

Biology 1/2 S

Softball practice 2 PE

Voice practice 1/2 FA

Glory (movie) 2 SS

IL=Independent Living Skills; SS=Social Studies; M=Math; FA=Fine Arts; S=Science; LA=Language Arts; and so on.

The listing should take the student no more than five minutes each morning. Using abbreviations speeds up the process.

Monthly, or more often if you prefer, convert the daily data into credits. As an example, create a Language Arts page, and list all the monthly hours devoted to Language Arts, together with short descriptions.

One of Tamara's monthly language arts pages looks like this:

LANGUAGE ARTS	HOURS
Reading	
Anne of Green Gables	6
Bible (Proverbs)	2
Animal Farm	2
Film	
Romeo and Juliet	2
Writing	
Correspondence	2
4-H Newsletter Article	6
4-H Descriptive Speech	4
Grammar lessons	4

55

Speaking
   4-H Speech Practice   <u>2</u>
                                   30 hours

We adopted the convention of assigning one high school credit to 120 hours of work, the equivalent of a year-long high school course. We broke down broad categories into smaller ones, which we then renamed as specific classes. For example Independent Living included Consumer Math, Careers, Home Economics, and Gardening. Social studies included History, Geography, Current Events, and Economics. Refer to Appendix K for more detail.

Recovering Lost Data

Do not despair if your teen has completed part of high school and you lack these records. Two states where we homeschooled, Colorado and New Mexico, mandated only that homeschoolers keep attendance and immunization data. And that is all we did. As we learned, you can recoup. It is work, but we did it and you can do it too. With our second child, we benefited from the knowledge that writing a transcript proceeds more smoothly with continuously maintained records.

To complete Jeff's transcript, we reconstructed what we thought had happened. For example, Jeff completed the *Saxon Algebra II* book. We knew he had spent at least 1-1/2 hours on each lesson and problem set and at least 1/2 hour on each test. Considering the number of lessons and tests, we totaled the hours spent on the course. It came out much higher than 120 hours, so we assigned 1 credit.

Another example. Tamara played board and computer geography games two times weekly, at least one hour each session. In addition, she read and discussed the newspaper for half an hour each day. This translated into at least 5 hours weekly, 20 hours monthly. After six months, she earned one credit, 120 hours time on task, in World Geography.

When you record daily academics and activities, you will be amazed how much "school" work teenagers do. Hiking becomes physical education. Stamp collecting is history and geography. Movies like *Apollo 13* and *Gettysburg* are history. Child care is home economics. Traveling becomes geography and economics. Computer games like *Sim City* are geography and critical thinking. Recording all activities—not just academics—creates data for impressive home-brew transcripts.

Reading Lists

Also, consider maintaining a reading list. The reading list is just that: an inventory of everything the student reads. We had our teenagers list author, title, and a rating 1–10 (1 being "so bad I could not finish it," 10 being just the opposite, "so good, I will re-read it many times."). We did not restrict our kids to age- or grade-appropriate materials, but instead encouraged them to read whatever they found interesting.

You need not include all reading in your teenager's final college application. Maintaining a log generates enough data to create an impressive list, though. Many selective colleges request either a senior year or a junior-senior year reading list. See Appendix A for part of Tamara's senior year reading list.

Documentation

In addition to recording activities and maintaining a reading list, retain documents that support your records. Here are some examples of supporting documentation:

- Work samples

- Awards

- Programs

- Published work

- Youth activity (4-H, etc.) brochures

- Job descriptions

- Photos

- Practice logs

- Team sports orientation sheets

- Music lesson information brochures

- Rating sheets from competitions

- Course descriptions

- Audio and video tapes

- External transcripts (issued by independent study programs and colleges)

- Standardized test results

- Letters of recommendation

You will not need all of the above documents. Just remember that thinking ahead and saving these materials makes putting together a college application much easier.

Letters of Recommendation

Letters of recommendation provide external validation of the homeschool transcript or portfolio, and as such are particularly important. Like standardized test results, letters of recommendation provide admissions officers with independent evaluations of an applicant's abilities and potential.

Homeschooled students should request letters of recommendation from any adult with whom they work for any length of time—a day to more than a year. Who are these adults? 4-H and Scout leaders, church leaders and choir directors, volunteer program directors, employers, coaches, music and dance teachers, homeschool support group leaders, tutors, and others.

Begin requesting letters in grade eight. This is not too early. Some of the student's eighth grade activities may become part of the high school transcript, particularly for those homeschoolers who complete high school ahead of schedule. Also, people move and forget. It is much easier to get good recommendation letters when the adult is working with the student rather than backtracking to obtain the letters several years later.

Occasionally an adult who is enthusiastic about a student will seem reluctant to write a letter of recommendation. Some do not like to write. Others are not sure exactly how to word the letter. Some simply do not have time. Of course, it is always best to have the letter in the adult's own words. However, if that is not possible, offer to do it for them. Yes, offer to write the letter. Make the recommender's task easy. Then he can simply review a draft, suggest changes, and sign it.

There are three essential components of letters of recommendation. First comes a statement describing the adult's experience with the student. Examples are: "I have coached Jeff as a member of the diving team for two years," or "As director, I have had the privilege of working with Tamara in the church choir."

The second component, the most important part of the letter describes skills, accomplishments, and character traits. "In his activities with Civil Air Patrol, Jeff has developed as a promising leader and a team player." "Tamara's enthusiasm for new tasks and her ability to communicate well with patients are assets to the hospital volunteer program." Ideally the body of the letter provides concrete examples to support general observations.

Third, the letter should include the actual recommendation. "It is with great pleasure that I recommend Jeff to your college." This statement, or a similar one, makes a strong beginning. Alternatively, it can be used to sum up, to complete the letter.

Turning Records into Transcripts

From a homeschooling perspective, there are two types of transcripts: external and home-brew. Umbrella schools, independent study schools, private and government high schools, and colleges all grant external transcripts. Homeschooling families write home-brew transcripts.

The home-brew document we developed is a master transcript. As such, it reflects our teenagers' entire educational experience. The master transcript includes data from all the external transcripts together with subjects covered at home. Jeff's transcript lists courses from Desert-Mountain Homeschool, American School, Community College of Aurora, and University of Denver. Tamara's transcript includes homeschool subjects together with courses from Overland High School, the local government school where she took choir and drama; Bendigo Senior Secondary School, which she attended as a foreign exchange student to Australia; and Wright State University. Appendix A includes copies of both transcripts.

Of course, college applications require official transcripts. The word "official" means only that the credit-granting institution issued the transcript. Even though we asked the correspondence high school and colleges to submit official transcripts, we attached non-official copies of those external transcripts to our master transcript. With a master transcript and its supporting documentation, colleges received everything at one time. They had all the data in one place. There was no need for them to piece together disparate information.

Successful homeschool transcripts follow many different formats. There is nothing particularly special about ours. I have seen courses listed by semester or simply by completion date. Some transcripts group courses according to department. For example, some group all science classes together. Others simply list courses alphabetically. In any case the format should be neat and easy to understand.

To determine what to include on our home-brew transcripts, we reviewed the high school transcripts of several friends. Most had social security numbers, so we listed social security numbers. They had lists of courses, so we had lists of courses. And so on. After reviewing more than ten transcripts, we found that all included the following information:

- Date issued

- Name and address of school

- Name and Social Security number of the student

- Names of completed and in-progress courses

This information is essential. As home educators, we also included descriptions of homeschooling courses.

The date issued on the transcript is the date the school or home-school sends the transcript to a college or other agency like a scholarship committee or insurance company. With my initial effort, Jeff's transcript, I did not specify the issue date, other than to show the period covered by the transcript at the top of the page. It is more in keeping with institutional practice to state the issue date as part of the header (see Tamara's transcript in Appendix A)

Note the name and address of the school near the top of the transcript. If you have not given your homeschool a name, consider doing so. Use any moniker that appeals to you—the street where you live, a favorite phrase, an historic figure, or a geographic feature of your community. Examples are Eagle's Nest Academy, Washington Preparatory School, Nelson's Ridge School, La Escuelita. We became Desert-Mountain Homeschool in Albuquerque, New Mexico.

The only controversy seems to be whether or not to include the word "homeschool." Even though we used the term, arguments for omitting it are valid. Some say that having the word homeschool on your letterhead and transcripts may cause confusion and raise unnecessary questions.

Of course your transcript will need the student's name plus another identifier to differentiate between individuals with the same name. You could use a birth date or mother's maiden name as the secondary identifier. Most colleges, however, prefer the Social Security number. Often that number or some portion of it becomes the student identification number.

During the application process, you will find it convenient to include student identifying information plus the school name and transcript issue date on each page. As you can see by reviewing Jeff's and then Tamara's transcript, we devised a more sophisticated document the second time around. On Tamara's transcript, the repeated student identifiers appear in the header.

Names and descriptions of completed and in-progress courses will comprise the body of your transcript. Referring back to Appendix A, you will see that we listed subjects on the first two pages, followed by course descriptions. Course listing is fairly straightforward. You may group them by semester, by year, by subject, or by completion dates, the tack we took.

Wording course descriptions can be tricky. We shamelessly cribbed educationese from local high school course catalogs. Check out the Music Theory and Appreciation course descriptions in Appendix A. We also referred to textbook introductions and to educational marketing materials. We derived our homeschool math course descriptions from information in Saxon Publishers' marketing brochures.

Chapter headings in books provided helpful data (see Jeff's Radio Electronics course description). We derived Tamara's course descriptions for when she was an exchange student in Australia from her recollections and explanations of what she studied there.

Optional transcript data includes:

- Grades (A-F/percents/pass-fail) and explanation of the grading system

- Credits and explanation of the credit-granting system

- Dates of courses taken or completed

- Grade point average (GPA)

- Standardized test scores

- Reading list

Grades and Grade Point Averages

We chose to attach grades and credits to the courses. On the flip side, homeschooled applicants have succeeded by simply listing and describing courses without credits or grades. Although you can say grades and credits are optional, do note that financial aid offices often need grade point averages to qualify applicants for federal financial aid.

If you list grades, define them on the transcript. Grades can be percentages or letters (A, B, C, D, F). The percentages may define the grades (A=93-100%, B=85-92%, C=77-84%, etc.) or vice versa (90-100%=A; 80-89%=B, etc.). You may prefer a descriptive scale (A=Excellent, B=Good, C=Average, D=Passing, Below Average, F=Failure). Although it is not important exactly what definitions or percentages you chose, it is important to incorporate the definitions and to be clear and consistent.

For consistency, we adopted American School's criteria to explain the transcript credits (120 hours equals 1 credit). Nationwide, 1 credit generally corresponds to a one-year high school course. Various transcripts I have reviewed award one credit for anywhere from 90 to 210 hours. Again, the exact definition is not as significant as clarity and consistency. Some home educators ignore the "seat time" definition of high school credit. They give one credit when their teenager completes the equivalent of a year-long high school course, regardless of the time it takes.

If you decide to include a Grade Point Average (GPA), also explain how you computed the average. The most widely used system begins with A=4.0. With this method, assign grade points as follows: A=4.0, B=3.0, C=2.0, D=1.0, F=0. To obtain grade points for each course, multiply the course credit by the points. A one-credit course with an assigned grade of "A" would earn 4 grade-points. A two-credit course with an assigned grade of "B" would earn 6 grade points. Finally, add all the grade points, and divide the total grade points by the total number of credits to obtain the GPA. Some high schools award extra grade points for Advanced Placement and Honors courses (for example, A=5.0), allowing their students to generate GPA's in excess of 4.0.

Looks Are Everything

A word processor, which permits easy updates, is the weapon of choice for writing transcripts. And, of course, with a word processor, you can make a professional presentation. While you are not trying to fool anyone into confusing your homeschool with the high school down the street, you need to make certain that admissions officers take your information seriously. If you do not own a computer, it is probably worth the expense to pay someone else to format the transcript, to make it look pretty. When dealing with bureaucracies, presentation can be more than half the game.

Ideally, beginning in grade nine, compile information and generate a transcript once or twice yearly. Even though most teenagers will not use the transcript for college applications that early, it may prove to be useful in other situations, like obtaining lower driving insurance rates.

More importantly, the content and appearance of a transcript give you and your teenager a feel for how your homeschooling looks on paper. As mentioned previously, many students find the transcript motivating. Finally, beginning early makes the job of completing college applications—if not easy—at least not daunting.

Involve your teenager as much as possible in writing the transcript and course descriptions. Our transcripts were a family effort. Jeff and Tamara provided the raw material—records, course listings, and course descriptions. I was the organizer and the translator, converting everyday language into educationese. Terry and Jeff and Tamara, all possessing superior computer skills, created the final products.

In summary, keep it simple. Make your format clear and easy to understand. Creating a master transcript and appending copies of external transcripts puts all the information in one place. Define terms like credit and grade. Use outside sources to help you write course descriptions in educationese.

Avoid copying our format exactly. Why? Our teenagers succeeded, in part, because we designed their transcripts around them and their talents. Experiment with different formats until you have something that highlights your homeschoolers' strengths.

Above all, involve your sons and daughters. After all, it is their education. Certainly, organizing the information and writing a transcript is an educational experience in itself. Count it as part of your homeschooling. We called it Language Arts, Critical Thinking, and Math.

Chapter Highlights

Homeschoolers may use transcripts or portfolios to document high school activities and academics.

A home-brew master transcript includes information from correspondence courses, college courses, homeschool academics, and related activities.

High school transcripts work for all homeschooling approaches — school-at-home, unit study, unschooling, and eclectic.

Begin detailed record keeping, using a simple calendar system and a few file folders, by grade nine or earlier.

Letters of recommendation provide external validation of homeschooled teenagers' achievements.

Many acceptable formats exist for transcripts. Develop one that presents your college applicant in the best light.

CHAPTER VI

THE BEST FIT

Where should your homeschooled student apply to college? Is the educational philosophy of a school important? Which colleges offer the right amount of challenge? How do you locate unusual degree programs? Are certain colleges particularly appropriate for home-schoolers?

Many see the goal of college admission as winning admission to the best school. However, there is no one best school, certainly no one best school for all students. Harvard would be a waste of time for a budding commercial artist. Cal Tech is no place for a musician or athlete. The military academies would be an absurd choice for a young entrepreneurial fashion designer.

Instead, consider a more realistic objective. Look for colleges that offer your teenage homeschooler the best fit. All students should look for majors of interest and challenging yet workable academics. Additionally, many homeschoolers seek colleges with compatible world views. They look specifically for conservative Christian schools or liberal institutions.

The best fit includes finding the best financing. Sean Callaway, a private college admissions adviser, goes even further. He says that admission to any school is a two-step process, each step equally important. First, win admission. Second, qualify for financial aid.

Many parents and students assume that their local state colleges and universities will be the least expensive. If you proceed on that premise, you will miss great deals—places like Berea College in Kentucky, where students have all costs met through work-study and other programs. Some small liberal arts colleges offer attractive financial aid packages, making them less expensive than state schools. For more examples, check out Appendix G, "Colleges of Special Interest To Homeschoolers."

To find the best fit and the best deal, consider six factors—programs of study, location, educational philosophy, competitiveness, size, and cost—not necessarily listed in order of importance. One student may care more about location than anything else. A second may prefer a small, intimate college experience, regardless of location. Yet a third may rejoice to find an infrequently offered major. Careful review of all six factors will help the student decide where to apply.

College Now?

Before considering the six factors in detail, many families will want to assess both the appropriateness and the value of a bachelor's degree. It is possible to keep costs to a minimum and get a college education for less than $5,000. However, even with financial aid, most parents and students will spend in the five figures range for four years of college, $10,000 to more than $100,000.

This is a lot of money. Should your homeschooler use the money instead to pursue other endeavors? How about setting up a business, attending trade school, or completing an apprenticeship? Some students join the military as a logical jumping off point for training and further education. The current GI Bill program allows military enlistees to save for college and qualify for government matching funds.

What about teenagers who want to attend college but are unsure of their direction? And what about the student who wants to delay or defer college attendance? Some say there is no sense going to college without clear-cut goals. It makes even less sense to send a student to college who does not want to be there at all. After all, a college degree does not guarantee employment. Both situations demand careful consideration.

Two excellent books can help you and your teenager with this decision—*The Question Is College* by Herbert Kohl, and *What Color Is Your Parachute?* by Richard Bolles.

The Question Is College directs student exploration of college versus non-college preparation for various career fields. Kohl's book is "...an attempt to help youngsters, with the assistance of their parents, confront the question, 'What can I do with my life?' during the last two years of high school and after graduation." The book emphasizes helping teenagers identify meaningful work, with or without college.

Richard Bolles annually updates *What Color Is Your Parachute? A Practical Manual For Job Hunters and Career-Changers* to reflect changes in the job market. Intended for all ages, *Parachute* helps individuals articulate interests and discover vocations. For those who bypass or defer college, Bolles' book helps immensely with the job search.

Because a college education does correlate with increased lifetime income, some (not me!) argue that most young adults should try to obtain a bachelor's degree. Others argue that a college education is the logical capstone to a well-rounded education and for that reason, college makes sense even for those individuals unsure of their direction.

Your teenager can begin college without declaring a major field of study. At most colleges, students spend the first year or two completing basic subjects. These core courses or distribution requirements expose them to a variety of disciplines. Students explore options and, after a year or two, select a major. Those unsure of a major will want to avoid colleges with a narrow focus, for example, a music conservatory or a business school.

Courses of Study and Special Programs

There is no sense sending Johnny to the nearest state university if it does not offer programs that interest him. At the library, check Barron's *Profiles of American Colleges* (updated annually) and similar reference books to research colleges. These references contain detailed information, from 800 telephone numbers for college admissions offices to entrance requirements, courses of study, and special programs.

Barron's has a nationwide listing of colleges, by major, at the front of the book. If you look under a heading like Nursing, you will find 500–600 colleges listed. On the other hand, fewer than ten colleges nationwide offer Oceanography or Dance Education. Having a major in mind can easily narrow the college search at the onset. You avoid wasting time researching schools that will never be appropriate.

Additionally, your student may be looking for specific programs. Examples are Reserve Officer Training Corps (ROTC), accommodations for learning disabled students, internships, credit for work experience, three-year baccalaureate degrees, pass/fail options, student-designed majors, foreign exchanges, on-campus religious groups, and so on. Barron's *Profiles of American Colleges* contains indexes to help you locate these programs.

Location

Most college applicants carefully consider location. Just as with real estate, location matters because you cannot change it. Most students concern themselves with two factors—setting and distance from home.

Distance from home to school impacts finances. If you reside in a large metropolitan area and have one or more local colleges within driving distance, you should carefully consider them. Living expenses on college campuses in the 1999–2000 school year were running $4,000–$10,000 per year. Over four years, students living at home save a substantial sum.

If your student attends college far from home, consider that each 200 miles corresponds to a half-day drive. Many students attending school more than 500 miles away may pay for four or more round-trip airline tickets per year—Christmas, Thanksgiving, spring break, and summer. Attending a geographically distant school usually increases costs by at least $1,000 annually.

Additionally, settings of colleges affect the students. Some people demand rural areas while others love large cities. Many big city schools, originally occupying prime real estate, now find themselves in unpleasant or dangerous neighborhoods. Setting also determines opportunities. Generally, expect more internships and paying jobs at schools in large cities.

While colleges' brochures and catalogs yield insight into setting, visiting will best address the location issue. Prospective students should ask not only, "Is this the right educational opportunity?" but also, "Do I want to live in this environment at this distance from home for four years?"

Educational Philosophy and Administration

Colleges and universities are loosely or highly structured, conservative or liberal, secular or religious, intensely bureaucratic or highly personalized, multi-faceted or specialized. Some emphasize liberal arts like history, literature, philosophy, or art. Others focus on professional, vocational, and technical studies, like business, engineering, communications, and nursing. Some colleges require that all graduates complete a long list of distribution or general education requirements. Others require very little outside a student's major. Higher education in the United States is characterized by tremendous diversity.

Various resources can tell you about a college's educational philosophy and administrative practices. To begin, request view books and other promotional literature. These free brochures, designed to sell students on the school and its programs, often include telltale language. Phrases like "self-directed learning" and "student-devised programs" imply a more liberal campus than phrases like "rigorous undergraduate program" and "adherence to Christian ideals."

Don't expect objectivity in a view book. No college ever looks as good in person as the pictures in the view book. And no college ever runs as smoothly as their promotional literature implies.

The next most readily available information about the educational philosophy and general climate of a school are the many college review books, available at most libraries (Appendix J). These books contain not only the school's stated educational philosophy but also students' evaluations of how the philosophy actually works in practice. Reviews assess the general atmosphere on campus. Reviews also address questions like, "How hard is the work?" and "How receptive is the administration to new ideas?"

While none of these factors much concerned our son Jeff, daughter Tamara was very picky about the atmosphere of the college she would attend. She favored a collaborative, discussion-oriented teaching style. She wanted lots of individual attention. Above all, she wanted to attend a conservative institution that did not have a lot of rules for behavior. Even with reading and research, it was difficult to evaluate these factors at a distance.

During a visit, though, Tamara determined that one of the schools on her application list fit her perfectly. The view book and catalog indicated that the school operates on an honor system, without a lot of specific rules. Many schools like this are very liberal. Contrary to expectations, she discovered a conservative student body. For whatever reason, the college attracts that kind of student.

Try to schedule day or overnight visits. During these visits, prospective students attend one or more classes and see the living quarters first hand. They have an opportunity to preview teaching styles, the student body, and facilities. Applicants develop a feel for a place and determine if the college operates with a compatible educational philosophy. Ideally, students make these visits in their sophomore and junior years of high school, before completing applications. If this has been impossible, do visit before deciding to attend and sending your acceptance deposit.

Compile lists of questions in advance of visits. Applicants should address queries to current students as well as to administrative personnel. Consider these questions to help prospective students assess educational philosophy and administrative practices.

• Would you choose this college again? Why or why not?

- Describe the faculty.

- How difficult is grading?

- How big is your largest class?

- Is it difficult to get certain courses?

- How safe do you feel here?

- What is the best thing here?

- What is the worst thing here?

Consider two additional reading-between-the-lines methods to determine educational philosophy and administrative practices. First, review application requirements. Second, ask the administration what paperwork homeschoolers need to submit with the application.

Reviewing application requirements allows you to differentiate colleges and universities that appear similar. Some colleges require enough paperwork to force you to buy a copy machine. Others are content with basic application data and an essay. Some will place most of their emphasis on the interview. At others, numbers, that is test scores and grade point averages, determine who receives an acceptance letter.

I know of one homeschooled student with a very non-traditional background. He told college admissions officers he had a problem because as a homeschooler he had no transcript. He asked what paperwork to submit with his application and received the following responses from four different institutions.

- Send us copies of the table of contents of all the books you have studied.

- Write homeschooled, N/A (not applicable) over the self-reported high school grade section and tell us about home schooling in your essay.

- Homeschooling is really interesting, send what you can.

- What problem?

This student ended up attending the last college, the one that answered, "What problem?" He loves the campus and the school. Responses to his one query helped him choose a compatible institution.

Competitiveness

As discussed in Chapter II, most American colleges and universities are either non-competitive or only marginally competitive, terms that I lump into the category non-selective. Most homeschoolers, regardless of academic background, should have a good shot at getting into these schools. Generally, students will want to apply to at least one sure bet, one college or university certain to admit them.

To gain entrance into one of the more academically selective colleges and universities, your homeschooler must demonstrate that he can handle more challenging work. To compare applicants to selective colleges, admissions officers review transcripts or portfolios, essays, interviews, letters of recommendation, and awards. Above and beyond these documents, however, is a single number, a number that allows colleges to instantly compare all applicants. That number is a standardized test score (SAT I or ACT).

With data from students accepted the previous year, most colleges publish two helpful statistics: average standardized test scores and scores of those in the 25th-75th percentile. Students scoring in the 25th percentile have a higher score than 25 percent of students admitted. Students scoring in the 75th percentile have a higher score than 75 percent of students admitted. The 25th to 75th percentile constitutes the test score range of the middle 50 percent. Here are some examples for the Scholastic Aptitude Test. A perfect score on each part, verbal and math, is 800.

	SAT I Average		25-75th percentile	
	Verbal	Math	Verbal	Math
Harvard	670	715	620-720	680-770
Rhodes College	570	635	520-620	570-680
Texas A & M	491	578	430-550	510-640

Test scores, by themselves, do not tell the whole story. Nevertheless, with them you can quickly determine which institutions are likely to offer admission, and, at the same time, offer sufficient challenge. *The Fiske Guide To Colleges* and other review books list the middle 50% range of standardized test scores of admitted students. Generally, an applicant's score should fall in the 25-75 percentile of previously admitted students.

As an example, Jenny has an SAT I score of 570 Verbal, 600 Math, that is 570 for the verbal section, 600 for the math section. University of Miami, Florida (25-75 percentile range: 520-630 Verbal, 580-680 Math) will probably look favorably on her application. Admission to Rhodes College, Tennessee (25-75 percentile SAT ranges are 590-690 Verbal, 590-690 Math), although not precluded, would be less likely.

Jenny probably should avoid applying to colleges where her SAT score exceeds that of most of the students—unless she is looking for a full academic scholarship. Many, if not most small and medium-size private colleges and some public colleges want to increase the average standardized test scores of their freshman classes. To raise these averages, the colleges offer merit scholarships to a very few applicants whose standardized test scores are higher than that of most students admitted. The merit scholarships sometimes pay all tuition. If a student like Jenny applies to Stephens College, Missouri (average SAT

530 Verbal, 500 Math), she may find herself competing for a full-tuition scholarship.

The same principle applies with higher or lower scores. Find a school that typically accepts applicants with lower standardized test scores than your student's, and inquire about merit scholarships. The outcome could make your homeschooler's college years very affordable.

Size

Colleges and universities range in size from small (under 1,000 students) to medium (1,000-5,000 students) to large (5,000-10,000 students) to very large (over 10,000 students). Generally smaller institutions offer better student-faculty ratios and more individual attention. Smaller schools often have a more family-like atmosphere and demand more accountability. It is hard to blend into the crowd at a smaller school where teachers notice every student absence.

At larger schools, it is easy to disappear in the crowd. At big colleges and universities, students have to take more responsibility for their education. Often they will need to be more aggressive to get what they want. On the plus side, though, larger colleges offer a wider variety of majors and extracurricular activities. For this reason, applicants unsure of a major should put one or more large schools high on their lists. In addition, bigger colleges offer more special programs, like ROTC, accommodations for learning disabled students, and inter-collegiate sports, to name a few.

Financial Considerations

Of course, cost factors into everything, especially college. Do not make it your initial concern, however. Find schools that offer a good fit for your homeschooler. Why? Those colleges will offer him the best financial aid package.

Financial aid application forms are nationally standardized. High school counseling offices and colleges themselves supply the Financial Aid Form (FAF) and the Free Application for Federal Student Aid (FAFSA). Colleges use the information on these forms to award need-based financial aid, including scholarships, parent loans, student loans, and work-study grants. Generally, schools notify students of financial aid awards concurrent with acceptance.

Most colleges and universities also award non-need-based aid or merit scholarships to applicants with high grade point averages and impressive standardized test scores. Students who exhibit other evidence of superior achievement also compete for merit scholarships. Read all the colleges' brochures carefully to learn if your teenager meets eligibility requirements for these awards.

Most colleges also have special category scholarships available for students who meet certain criteria. Examples are "descendant of a Civil War veteran," or "woman majoring in physical therapy." Each college's financial aid office can provide information on these special scholarships.

Submit materials early to qualify for both need-based and non-need-based aid. Meeting deadlines is extremely important. Make certain that you always have appropriate forms on hand. Whenever you request general information from colleges and universities, request financial-aid and merit scholarship information at the same time.

College and university financial aid offices disperse most of the big money. Additionally, smaller, one-time awards may be available in your community. The two primary sources are employers and community groups. For example, because her father is on active-duty in the Air Force, Tamara applied for scholarships awarded to children of active-duty military officers at our current base. Check with your employer and your spouse's employer.

Also, check with community groups like churches, Rotary, Scouts, and the YMCA. You need not necessarily affiliate with these groups for your student to compete for scholarships, although it probably helps in some cases. Your local newspaper will generally include information on application procedures for these awards. In addition, check on locally awarded scholarships with nearby high school counseling offices. Or contact groups directly. Begin with those with whom you have affiliations.

The ROTC (Reserve Officer Training Corps) constitutes a special category of scholarship application. ROTC scholarships pay partial to all academic expenses plus a stipend. Students receiving these funds agree to serve in the United States Armed Forces upon graduation. While in college, ROTC students participate in military training on weekends and during the summer. ROTC students also take several military science classes during their college careers.

ROTC restricts scholarship eligibility to certain majors. Engineering, computer science, and nursing are the principal ones, but there are others. Obtain ROTC applications from military recruiters and from colleges that offer ROTC programs; there are separate ones for the Army, Navy, Marines, and Air Force.

Several colleges nationwide offer special financial inducements. Like the military academies, they offer a nearly all-expenses-paid education. "A Few Colleges of Special Interest to Homeschoolers," Appendix G, details some of these. For a complete list, see the current issue of *Money Magazine's Best College Buys Now*, available at newsstands each fall.

Discussing college financing in detail is beyond the scope of this book. Among the Resources listed in Appendix J, there are excellent materials devoted to meeting college costs. Learn about the process, keep in touch with college financial aid officers, and scout your community for local awards.

Paring Down The List

How many colleges should your teen apply to? First, consider the trade-off. Applications take time and cost money. Each application to a selective school requires another essay, more letters of recommendation, two or more hours of completing forms, and perhaps more interviews. For homeschooled students, each application means another session compiling and copying documents, the transcripts that traditionally-schooled students simply order from their high schools. In short, you need time and energy to do justice to each application.

Practically speaking, something in the neighborhood of three to six applications works well. Include a sure bet college, one that typically accepts students with fewer qualifications than your teen has. Depending on circumstances, you may want to include one or two long shots, schools whose selectivity seems to place them out of reach.

Always look for the best fit and a good deal. Information is all around you, free for the asking. Most localities offer college fairs in late summer or early fall at various locations—malls, public convention centers, colleges, and high schools. Your local newspaper will usually list dates and times. Or contact public and private high school counseling offices for college fair information.

Colleges send representatives to these fairs to distribute information, answer questions, and—most particularly—to sell you on their college. They want to meet prospective applicants and parents, so do not be intimidated. Attend with your teenager, or send him alone. Asking intelligent questions improves homeschoolers' images, so go prepared!

Many colleges have toll free telephone numbers, and all now have web sites. Barron's and other library college reference books list contact phone numbers and Internet addresses. Call and ask for general information, brochures about specific programs, financial aid information, and applications. After reviewing the information, students should call colleges back and ask specific questions. Most selective schools keep track of these calls. Again, students' demonstrated interest positively factors into the admissions process.

Initial information requests usually place your teen on colleges' mailing lists. This is a good thing. Colleges often send representatives to medium and larger-sized metropolitan areas to give short presentations and to answer questions about their school. They notify students on the mailing list of these visits in advance. Ideally, students should be on these mailing lists by the end of their sophomore year in high school.

Other excellent sources of information about a given college or university include current students and alumni of the school. You may know someone among your circle of neighbors, friends, co-workers, and relatives who can give you the inside scoop on everything from the academic intensity to the social scene.

In addition, explore Usenet discussion groups and homeschooling discussion boards on the Internet. I personally host a high school/college discussion board at Kaleidoscapes, (www.kaleidoscapes.com/colleges.htm). If you have Internet access—and most of us do, at local libraries—the World Wide Web provides informational listings on many colleges and universities (see Appendix J).

Chapter Highlights

Look for The Best Fit, not the best college.

College is not the best choice for everyone. All teenagers should assess whether or not a college degree will further their goals.

Library research can help you find the best college fit with respect to academics, special programs, size, cost, location, and educational philosophy.

Supplement library research with campus visits and interviews of current and former students.

CHAPTER VII

PUTTING IT ALL TOGETHER

This is it—the final leg of the journey. You and your teenager have narrowed down the college choices and requested applications. Your file folders bulge with papers documenting academic and non-academic accomplishments. Your homeschooler has his SAT I or ACT scores. You have written a customized transcript, and your teenager is ready to compose a résumé. Now for the grand finale—putting it all together and completing three to six college applications.

Crossing The T's, Dotting The I's

College applications include several forms plus requests for various documents like transcripts, letters of recommendation, essays, and so on. Admissions personnel use forms to make life easy for the vast majority of applicants, students who attend schools and participate in typical school-related activities. Of course, these forms facilitate admissions officers' evaluations and expedite review.

Unfortunately, parts of some standardized forms present difficulties for home educators. Examples are questions about class rank or typical high school activities like football team, cheer leading, band, class offices, and French club. Homeschooled applicants also find counselor recommendation forms, English and math teacher reports, and high school extracurricular forms inapplicable to their educational background.

Obviously, typical forms included with most blank applications were not designed for homeschoolers. Nevertheless, some homeschooling parents read the forms and begin to focus on "holes." Most homeschooled teenagers never worked on the yearbook, ran for class office, or lettered in a high school sport. If your teenager cannot check any of the high school extracurricular form boxes, there must be huge gaps. Right? Wrong.

A form may ask about holding a class office or participating in band. That does not mean your student needs experience with these specific activities to receive favorable consideration. Most home-schoolers have unusual backgrounds including different activities. Unusual does not mean worse. In many cases, admissions personnel view unique activities favorably. The challenge lies in presenting homeschooling positively and clearly. See your glass as half full rather than half empty and communicate that vision to admissions officers.

With the counselor and teacher forms, we did one of two things. Either I filled them out, as the counselor or teacher, or I wrote across them, "Not Applicable—Homeschooled student—see cover letter." Sometimes I guessed wrong. On one of Jeff's ROTC scholarship applications, I wrote "N/A, see cover letter," on the math and English teacher forms. They sent them back, insisting that the forms had to be completed, regardless of the circumstances. Okay, no problem. I completed them as the math teacher, as the English teacher. I can only imagine the reviewer's raised eyebrows when I explained that Jeff had no English or math teacher, and that he taught himself these subjects.

Some portions of applications will not make sense in a home-schooling context. An example is class rank. Just write, "Homeschooled student—not applicable," in or near this blank. Do the same for any other information that does not apply. Or tickle someone's funny bone. Your student is one out of one, first in his class of one!

To convey an accurate picture of our children, we created our own forms. As outlined in the first chapter, we developed and used three principal information organizing tools.

- Cover letter from me, the principal of Desert-Mountain Homeschool

• Home-brew master transcript

• Student résumé

Chapter V details the transcript. The next sections describe the cover letter and résumé. For the following discussion, refer to sample cover letters in Appendix B and sample résumés in Appendix C.

Cover Letter

Our cover letter served three purposes. Referring specifically to Jeff's cover letter (Appendix B), I first detailed his homeschooling background, listing the various components—independent study courses, college subjects, and homeschool courses. Second, I described one of Jeff's typical days to clarify our educational philosophy. Third, I addressed questions asked on the teacher and counselor report forms, making the cover letter a partial substitute for missing counselor and teacher recommendations. Letters of recommendation from Jeff's coaches and Civil Air Patrol senior members and music teachers also filled this gap.

Cover letters may be written by parents, students, or both. Of course, if the student authors the cover letter, using the letter as a substitute for the counselor and teacher recommendations is not an option. On the other hand, I have read some very impressive student-authored cover letters, letters that would make me want to accept the applicant without further review.

We placed the cover letter immediately behind the application form, in front of all other material. At the outset, the admissions staff would see the outlines of an unusual, nevertheless well-thought-out situation.

In the cover letter, I explained the components of homeschooling by describing how and where Jeff had earned his high school credits. As explained previously, he had credits generated at home, as well as credits from an independent study high school and two colleges.

Some of the homeschool credits (Radio Electronics, Piano Performance) resulted from activities, as opposed to formal coursework. I described how the home-brew master transcript summarized this information.

By describing one of Jeff's days, we gave colleges an inside peek at our homeschool and discussed our educational philosophy at the same time. Remember that most admissions personnel, just like most of the general population, have no immediate experience with home education. A concrete approach to your educational philosophy will help them put it in perspective.

More than one admissions officer I interviewed said that a family's reasons for homeschooling mattered a great deal. An admissions officer at Rice University wanted assurance that families of applicants had reviewed their options and selected the best education available. Interestingly—and inappropriately, I think—he also questioned any family who chose to homeschool in a district with an excellent reputation, such as Fairfax County, Virginia. Only very compelling reasons could justify homeschooling in such an environment, in his opinion.

To communicate your educational philosophy, consider devoting part of your cover letter to one of two items. Either discuss how you got started homeschooling, a story you have undoubtedly told many times. Or describe a typical day for your homeschooled teenager. With both approaches, conclude by discussing how and why you homeschool. For obvious reasons, avoid negative comments on institutional schooling. After all, it is probably not formal education most homeschoolers oppose, just bad formal education.

Finally, your cover letter can substitute for teacher and counselor reports. If it does, be sure to address questions asked on those forms. Generally, teacher and counselor forms request commentary on the student's initiative, motivation, creativity, self-discipline, leadership, emotional maturity, and so on. We found that questions did differ enough from college to college to warrant customized cover letters, so I wrote separate letters to each school to which our children applied.

Résumé

The résumé, like the cover letter, served more than one purpose. First, the résumé allowed us to include things that were not appropriate for the transcript and did not fit elsewhere on the application. Second, Jeff and Tamara provided résumés to interviewers and others who would be writing recommendations.

As discussed previously, most applications to selective colleges include one or more forms to report participation in extracurricular activities. These may include athletic activities, school offices, school publications, musical groups, youth organizations, and awards and honors.

Homeschooled students generally have a full slate of outside interests. Examples include volunteer and paying work; individual sports like gymnastics, Tae Kwon Do, and distance running; and private music lessons and recital performances. Homeschoolers' résumés list things like published writing, computer programming, and running a business.

How can you fit this onto an application with check-off boxes keyed to typical high school activities? For our teenagers' applications, we completed the forms, and we wrote "N/A—see résumé," in appropriate places. In some instances, we simply wrote "N/A—see résumé," across the entire form.

For example, one form requested information about music participation, yet only allowed the student to check off band, chorus, or orchestra. Other parts of the form were just as inappropriate. We wrote "N/A—see résumé," across the entire form. When the reviewer referred to the résumé, they saw that Jeff had taken piano lessons, participated in music competitions, taught piano, and performed in recitals.

Because we organized our résumés to emphasize each student's strengths, we used different categories for two very different people, Jeff and Tamara. We divided Jeff's résumé into education, activities, and awards. Tamara's résumé headings are education, activities, work experience, volunteer experience, and awards. Similarly, customize your résumé headings to your teenagers. Experiment with various categories until you have outlines that accurately and favorably portray their accomplishments.

We submitted each résumé with supporting documentation. We attached letters from music teachers and coaches and copies of award certificates. Jeff's documentation included his private pilot and amateur radio logs as well as his amateur radio license. Tamara's application contained church bulletins detailing her work with younger children. Both had samples of articles written for various newsletters. Any time we could include documentation, we did so.

The résumés turned out to be more useful than we had anticipated. Jeff originally wrote his résumé to complement his applications. As we accidentally discovered, however, the résumé also proved helpful to interviewers and others who wrote letters of recommendation for Jeff.

Students applying to selective colleges and for scholarships at any college often interview with individuals and committees who have never met them before. The interview, one in a long procession, may last ten or fifteen minutes. The interviewers write recommendations and reports, and these documents become part of the student's college application.

Submitting a copy of the résumé during the interview ensures that interviewers will remember details of the student's background. It also increases the likelihood that interviewers will notice items not discussed. It was expensive to fly Jeff to Texas to interview with our congressman's office for his academy nominations. We are talking about a two-day trip and overnight stay, all for a 15-minute interview. Leaving a résumé with the nominating committee made the trip seem more worthwhile.

Jeff also gave the résumé to any adult from whom he requested a letter of recommendation. Usually the writer knew him in a single capacity, say as a Civil Air Patrol cadet or a member of the diving team. Supplying the résumé made the recommender's task easier by providing more data. The résumé also furnished ready-made phrases to help the writer articulate the student's accomplishments.

Application Essay

Selective colleges and universities, as part of their applications, ask for one or more student essays. Essay topics run the gamut from general to specific. Here are some common examples.

- Write a brief statement of your academic goals.

- What social or political issue most concerns you and why?

- What is the most significant event in your life?

- Make up your own essay question and answer it.

According to a *Washington Post* article (December 5, 1999) titled, "Essays on Elvis: Colleges Stretch, Stress Applicants," some colleges have begun to ask creative or nightmarish essay questions, depending on your point of view. Examples from the article include the following.

- Name something with extraterrestrial origins. Offer a thorough defense of your hypothesis.

- What is your favorite word and why?

- Can a toad hear? Prove it.

In addition, many schools now give students the option of choosing their own topics.

Regardless of the question, most good essays relate to concrete events in the student's life. To develop material for an essay, I encourage all high school homeschoolers to keep a daily or weekly journal. In the journal, students record events and activities together with their impressions. This need not be a major project, just five to ten minutes of writing each day or ten to twenty minutes of writing once per week.

When it comes time to write the essays, the student reviews his journal, looking for experiences that relate to application questions. Of course, at this point, the journal contains a wealth of material— book and movie reviews, family and community anecdotes, and descriptions of special projects. Most students with journals have little trouble recalling events to address almost any application question.

Regardless of the topic, students should allow more than a month to write the essay. Both Jeff and Tamara re-wrote their application essays several times before showing them to anyone. They then completed additional drafts based on comments from several adults. Appendix D contains examples of two of these essays. My web site— www.homeschoolteenscollege.net—has additional essays, written by other homeschoolers. We found The Princeton Review's *The Student Access Guide To College Admissions* chapter on application essays an invaluable aid.

Common Application

Applications, especially those to selective colleges and universities, are a lot of work. As a result, an increasing number of schools accept the Common Application. The Common Application is exactly what it sounds like—a single form that a large number of colleges have agreed to accept instead of their own form.

According the Michele Hernandez in *A Is For Admission,* the common application was developed to help disadvantaged applicants. She writes that use of the common application handicaps most applicants to very selective colleges. The common application requires one essay rather than two or three, and it does not ask for AP scores.

Ms. Hernandez, a former Ivy League admissions officer, also tells us that too often reviewers find it difficult to assess common application information. Except for those very economically disadvantaged—the group for whom the common application was developed—she urges applicants to selective colleges to use the school's regular application.

Of course, the Common Application makes applying to college much less time consuming. The student completes one application, not several. He sends photocopies to all the colleges to which he is applying that accept it. Homeschoolers applying to a string of sure-bet colleges may want to consider using it. Obtain the Common Application through high school guidance counselors or through any of the colleges and universities that use it.

Deadlines

Meeting deadlines is extremely important. Missing them costs money and results in lost opportunities. Colleges charge late fees. Applicants can sacrifice eligibility for financial aid programs and merit scholarships. Missing deadlines often disqualifies students from honors and other special programs. Turning in late paperwork even affects the availability of on-campus housing.

To avoid problems caused by missing deadlines, homeschooled juniors and seniors should keep a deadline calendar. On the calendar the student notes due dates for standardized test registrations, test reports to colleges, application submissions, medical reports, interviews, and scholarship and financial aid forms.

In this vein, note also that many selective colleges and universities accept early decision applications. Early decision means that your student applies only to his first choice school. If the college admits him, they will notify him early enough, usually in December, so that he will not have to file other applications. Early decision application deadlines precede normal deadlines by one to three months.

Many non-selective colleges use rolling admissions. With rolling admissions, the college or university accepts applications for the fall term any time the previous winter, spring, and summer, until all places are filled. Colleges using rolling admissions do not guarantee acceptance. These schools do fill up, so file these applications promptly, as well.

With good records, it is possible to complete an application to many non-selective schools in an evening. In contrast, be sure to allow plenty of time for submissions to selective institutions. Figure three months for standardized tests. Register six weeks in advance, and receive score reports six weeks after taking the test. External transcripts can take a month or more. Good essays take several days, at least. Allow several weeks to request and obtain recommendation letters.

It is a lot to monitor. Appendix I, "A Homeschooler's College Planning Checklist," can help you meet deadlines. It includes items that our family and others overlooked, until it was too late. Read it and revise it to fit your situation.

The Product

The final form of each of our student's applications included the following documents, in the order listed.

- College forms

- Cover letter

- Desert-Mountain Homeschool Transcript

- Desert-Mountain Homeschool Course Descriptions

- Copies of external transcripts

- Résumé

- Documentation of résumé items

- Letters of recommendation

- Student essay

- Copies of standardized test score reports

You will compile something similar, subject to the varied requirements of different colleges. Before mailing, make complete copies for your files. Try to submit materials well in advance of deadlines.

Colleges and universities usually request that external transcripts and standardized test scores be submitted directly by the educational institution or testing agency. Even though we arranged to have this done, we felt that submitting copies of external college transcripts with the applications presented a clearer, easier-to-review picture of our teenagers. In cases where outside agencies were particularly slow in sending transcripts, submitting the copies probably expedited the review process.

Chapter Highlights

College application forms do not show off homeschoolers in the best light. Therefore, supplement with cover letters and résumés.

Cover letters substitute in part for high school counselor recommendations and give families an opportunities to explain why they homeschool.

Résumés can take the place of high school activity forms. Résumés also fill in the blanks for those writing letters of recommendation and interview reports for homeschoolers.

Draw examples for application essays from student journals.

Use a college-planning checklist to meet deadlines.

CHAPTER VIII

COLLEGE AT HOME

Sarah, age 15, has decided to continue homeschooling through high school. She and her parents have discussed goals and priorities and created a list of activities.

Sarah, like an increasing number of homeschooled teenagers, has included two college classes on her list, biology and Latin. Because the closest college is 45 minutes distant, Sarah plans to take these courses at home, one through correspondence, the other on-line.

Sarah dreams of becoming a veterinarian. She raised sheep as a project for her 4-H club and uses the family microscope to learn elementary cellular biology. Her background also includes applying concepts of basic botany in the family garden, working with an animal rescue group, and reading widely about botany, biology, and veterinary medicine. She and her parents reviewed the course content of typical high school biology classes by examining textbooks at the library. They agreed—the high school material was too elementary, and she could probably handle college-level biology.

So—also at the library—Sarah and her parents perused *The Independent Study Catalog: A Guide To Over 10,000 Correspondence Courses* by Peterson's Guides. It lists more than thirty independent study institutions offering introductory college biology, among them the University of Kansas and the University of Kentucky. Both schools allow high school students to enroll in college courses for credit. Not only can Sarah take college biology as a 15-year-old homeschooler, she has a choice of programs, allowing her family to shop for quality and price.

Sarah and her parents also know that foreign language study will enhance her college applications, so, with a little computer research, they discover The Internet University (www.caso.com), a site that catalogs on-line courses. Thinking that college introductory Latin probably closely resembles high school introductory Latin (and it does, except that college Latin covers twice as much ground in a year), she chooses a college course. Why not earn college credit now?

Sarah, like many teenage homeschoolers, is part of a growing phenomenon known as distance learning (DL). Distance learning means that instructors and students seldom or never meet face to face. Geographically separated, they live across town, and more frequently in different cities and different states. In addition to college at home, distance learning includes individual courses for grades K-12; high school diploma programs; and associate's, bachelor's, master's, and doctoral programs.

Businesses, government agencies, and non-profit organizations also offer distance learning courses. These programs are incredibly varied, from repairing antique dolls to medical transcription to computer repair to indexing books.

Why such an explosion of options for distance education? First, student demographics are changing. There are more older, return-to-schoolers, as well as more homeschoolers. Second, all colleges and universities are competing for students. Multiplying services by offering distance learning increases enrollment. Finally, advances in telecommunications have turned the stodgy, matchbook-cover-advertised correspondence course into the high-tech solution to twenty-first century educational challenges.

Reasons To Consider Distance Education

- **Independence.** Some teenage homeschoolers share several traits of successful distance learners. They are highly motivated and accustomed to independent study. They like working at their own pace, on an individualized timetable.

- **Flexibility.** Homeschoolers, just like older working parents who comprise so much of the DL population, love the flexibility distance education affords. Class and study time are not restricted to Monday through Friday 8-5, but instead fit in and around the student's activities, travel plans, and work schedule.

• **Accomodating younger students.** Distance learning allows children to take college classes at younger ages than local colleges in some states currently permit. I encounter homeschoolers like Sarah often. These teenagers excel in one or more subjects, and their level of expertise and motivation warrant college-level instruction.

• **Impressing admissions officers and qualifying for big-money scholarships.** A's and B's in college classes, whether DL or not, may mean as much or more than scoring high on Advanced Placement and SAT II (Achievement) Tests. Admissions officers recognize this. After all, high AP and SAT II scores merely predict college success—and some critics question even this. Completing college courses concurrent with high school exceeds this standard by demonstrating college success.

• **Natural continuation of home education.** An increasing number of homeschoolers, after finishing high school studies, choose distance learning, the college at home format, for all or part of a 2-year associate's or 4-year bachelor's degree. Homeschooling has worked well for them; and they simply continue, homeschooling college.

• **Access to a wide variety of courses.** Taking college classes at home allows teenagers to explore subject areas not offered at local high schools or colleges. Those with an interest in oceanography or historic preservation or dance therapy can pursue their special interests and generate college credit, regardless of the offerings at the local colleges.

• **Paper trails.** Many distance learning programs offer credit-generating alternatives, all attractive to homeschoolers. For example, students may self-instruct American History with methods and resources they choose. When they complete the material, they take a test for college credit. Other students compile portfolios, detailing, for example, special projects for computer science or art credits. Similarly, some colleges accept Red Cross First Aid and CPR courses for science credit. Our son's amateur radio license may have gotten him some electronics and communications credit at colleges with alternative credit generating programs. While traditional school settings offer some of these options, distance learning programs provide these opportunities more often. These alternatives attract homeschoolers who prefer a more collaborative and hands-on approach to education.

• **Techno-advantages.** Distance education offers an interface that is very attractive to some homeschoolers, namely computer-mediated learning. More than one homeschooling parent has told me how much his teenager accomplishes even with boring computer programs. From others I hear stories of writing prowess developed solely because of word-processing technology or on-line bulletin boards. Their teenagers excel by cozying up to a computer screen.

• **Personal enrichment.** Like some senior citizens with no thoughts of studying for a degree, some teenagers and young adults take ancient Greek or art appreciation for fun. Or they study computer science or accounting to help build a business. DL affords them the opportunity to explore their interests, no matter how eclectic or specialized. Their freedom to explore can open the door to unexpected fields and careers.

• **Reducing college costs.** Finally, while college at home is not free, it can be less expensive than traditional college for two reasons, one obvious, the other not. As pointed out previously, reducing living costs by remaining at home decreases overall college costs by one-third to one-half. In addition, those taking college classes concurrent with high school homeschooling earn college credit earlier.

Because costs are always rising, earlier credit is usually cheaper credit.

Thorns In The Roses

College at home, like a rose, smells sweet but has its share of thorns. There is a downside.

• **Discipline.** The first disadvantage hits most when they sit down with their first correspondence or computer distance learning course. Independent study, including setting your own schedule, takes discipline. Many people need the live teacher, scheduled assignments, examinations, and even peer pressure to succeed.

• **"Are we done, yet?"** College at home can be boring. I-teach/you-learn instructional formats often generate this criticism. While some independent study programs are so well tuned that the courses are more interesting than classes at the state university, others are as dry as yesterday's toast.

• **Unavailability.** It is impossible to complete college at home in some career fields. I have yet to find a piano performance degree, the student-teacher part of teacher certification, or practical nursing training in a distance learning format.

• **Facilities.** Students on most college campuses have access to a library and computer facilities. Distance learners may find their personal and local resources inadequate. For some distance-learning programs, students need a TV and VCR, or a FAX machine. For others, access to a good library is essential.

• **Transferring credits.** Distance learning college credit may or may not be accepted by another college's two-year or four-year degree program. You are most likely to encounter this problem with very selective colleges like Harvard, Brown, Yale, Rice, Stanford, and

MIT. But it can be a problem at less selective institutions. Certainly check with any four-year college your student may eventually attend on campus if credit transferability concerns you. To further complicate matters, some colleges refuse to transfer credit for any DL or other college courses if the credit counts for both high school graduation and college credit. Families writing their own transcripts can work around this by stating that college classes were not used to satisfy their high school diploma requirements. Those relying on external high school transcripts that show college credits as partial satisfaction of high school requirements need to proceed with caution. Again, check with targeted colleges about this. In some cases, homeschooling families will want to balance the non-transferability of credit with the advantages of showing college credit on a high school transcript. You may not care about transferability if the college course credit helps your student win a full scholarship or admission to a very selective school.

• **Traditional college perks.** Finally, an on-campus college experience offers more than information. It offers people—professors, visiting lecturers, and other students as well as a variety of resources, such as video labs and extracurricular activities. While campus life is not for everyone, it has great appeal for some students as well as distinct advantages for certain specialized fields. Aspiring set designers, actors, or archeologists, for example, need contacts in their fields and hands-on experiences. On campus attendance provides one way, although not the only way, to find them. On the other hand, homeschoolers accustomed to finding their own resources may be able to get more real-world experience in the larger community than they could get on a college campus.

Distance Learning Instructional Formats

So what, exactly, is distance education? How are college at home courses delivered and what types of credit options exist?

The oldest mode of distance education is correspondence. Think "college course in a box," with the college providing text, syllabus, outline, lectures, assignments, and other materials. Students complete assignments and mail them back to the instructor for grading.

Current distance learning incorporates telephone communication as well as broadcast and recorded media. For example, foreign language programs may be taught with daily instructional TV programming. Hands-on projects and interactive exchanges characterize most second-generation college at home programs. Students find themselves using local libraries and other community resources as well as discussing questions and projects over the telephone with instructors and sometimes with other students. Newer DL programs emphasize collaboration. Students may contribute to course content and design, working out ways to obtain credit for hands-on projects, volunteer work, and paying jobs.

On-line distance learning is the newest player on the college at home field. But beware. The words "on-line college course" can mean almost anything, as described in the following paragraphs.

On-Line Distance Education

College A has an on-line program. They assign work and encourage dialogue with instructors via e-mail. Otherwise all course materials arrive by mail, and instruction is traditional with textbooks, assignments, and grades. Provisions for student interaction are nonexistent.

College B conducts asynchronous classes, in which students begin classes anytime and work at their own pace. Students receive lessons and send completed assignments via e-mail. The program provides electronic discussion boards or e-mail loops, for public discussions between students and instructors or among the students themselves.

College C does all of the above and adds synchronous classes, in which students read the material and do associated projects at roughly the same time. For example, the third week in March, all students will read the same lesson and receive the same writing assignment. College C incorporates the World Wide Web (www), encouraging on-line as well as more traditional research.

College D provides all of the above—e-mail, Internet research assignments, discussion boards—and schedules real-time classes, wherein participants take the classes not just the same week, synchronously, but at the same time of day. These programs—still fairly rare—emphasize real time interaction via an on-line classrooms or chat rooms.

Currently, in the United States, the majority of on-line college courses are asynchronous. Students begin courses at any time of year and proceed at their own pace. They may occasionally interact with other students via an Internet bulletin board or an e-mail loop. In addition, many of the schools providing on-line college at home include video and audio materials, laboratory supplies, test-out options, and credit for non-traditional work.

To sum up, the term "on-line" means many things. There are different modes of course delivery, depending on the level of technology used. When evaluating these programs, remember that many succeed with college at home without a computer. There are thousands of courses and hundreds of programs, whether you use the U.S. Postal Service or the most advanced telecommunications equipment.

"I get credit for that?"

Just as course delivery methods vary, programs vary. Some courses and programs are traditional—textbook, syllabus, test, grade. Other programs encourage students to "design your own study," for both individual courses and for associate's, bachelor's, and master's degrees.

For example, Ohio University in Athens, Ohio, offers individual learning contracts. From their literature: "The Associate In Independent Study is a self-designed degree; students are required to submit a proposal outlining their course of study and area of concentration." Ohio University currently offers more than 300 DL courses and has more than 3,000 students enrolled.

Many distance learning programs offer a plethora of credit-generating options. Take Thomas Edison State College, a state-supported, fully accredited school in New Jersey, with almost 2,000 students enrolled in distance education programs in 1996. They offer two-year Associate's and four-year Bachelor's degrees in more than 100 areas.

Enrollees at Thomas Edison State College get college credit for testing, portfolio reviews, certificates and licenses, and courses taken in other venues. Students may teach themselves trigonometry, with resources they choose, then simply take a test for credit. Others put together portfolios, detailing a special project for credit in computer science.

Smart Shopping

Remember that distance learning, especially college distance learning, is expanding rapidly, both in delivery modes and course offerings. That means that you need to telephone or write or browse the Internet to find current information.

Start locally. Contact the two-year junior colleges and four-year colleges and universities in your community and within your state and ask what independent study courses and programs they offer. The first person you reach, usually in admissions will probably refer you to another office. You will hear various department designations, among them independent study, extension, college at home, distance education, off-campus, and adult learning.

When you talk to the colleges, you will often learn that there are no minimal requirements for enrollment in basic classes. Some colleges require all incoming students take basic English and math assessment tests. Generally, these are not used to refuse admission, only to ascertain the student has the skills to succeed in courses he selects.

Some colleges will have age restrictions or require a GED or high school diploma. If this is the case, always ask about applying for a waiver, usually a simple procedure. Or—if appropriate—go ahead and grant your high school diploma or have your student take the GED. Or vote with your feet—check out other programs.

Next, visit the library for a little research. Here are my favorites:

Peterson's Independent Study Catalog: A Guide to Over 10,000 Correspondence Courses indexes independent study courses across the nation by subject area. They list over twenty schools that offer independent study geology courses, thirty that offer German. There are also short blurbs telling you about the policies of each school. For the University of Texas at Austin and Mississippi State University and many others, the policies include: "High school students may enroll in undergraduate courses for credit."

I also like *College Degrees by Mail and Internet* by John Bear and Mariah Bear. This book, updated frequently, contains brief descriptions of 100 accredited schools that offer bachelor's, master's, and doctorates. It also contains good discussions of how to evaluate programs and how to judge accreditation.

On-line, check out *The Internet University: College Courses by Computer* by Dan Corrigan (www.caso.com), which explains types of on-line academics and details thousands of course offerings.

In addition, to evaluate these programs, talk with working professionals in fields of interest. If your teenager is interested in journalism, does the editor of the local newspaper think an English or journalism degree from University A will do the trick? What does your tax preparer think of the accounting degree from College B? Network to find somebody working in the student's target field. Show this person the college at home course selections or degree program your student is considering, and ask if he thinks the program looks like good career preparation for that field. Have your homeschooler call the personnel departments of companies and government agencies whose work interests him and query them about the proposed college at home program.

As you compare offerings and prices, either for individual courses or degree programs, shop smart. Ask the school for personal references. Talk to people who have completed the courses or programs. Learn about withdrawal and refund policies. Ask to see sample materials. And, just as you would ask to sit-in on classes at a regular college, ask to preview on-line classes before you buy.

Finally, ask for statistics, the numbers, such as:

- How many people who enroll in the course or program complete it?

- What are the principal reasons—according to the college—for non-completion?

- What is the average completion time?

- Where are your graduates employed?

- How many went to graduate school? What schools?

Follow Through

Will college at home work for your teenager or your homeschool graduate? That depends on how your student's personality and interests mesh with his options. In that spirit, here is some sundry advice, gathered principally from discussions on various Internet bulletin boards, to increase the chances for success.

First, don't dive in, just dip your toes in the water. Try one course before you decide on multiple courses or a degree program. Many homeschooling parents urge their children to take courses in fields in which they and their teenagers have no expertise, exactly the wrong approach for that first distance learning course. Instead, try a subject where your student excels. If your teenager has difficulties with subject matter he likes, certainly college at home will not be appropriate for more challenging and perhaps less interesting material.

There is a second benefit to trying an "easy" class. Students already somewhat familiar with the subject matter of that first course are also in a better position to evaluate the content and quality of a college's distance learning program in general.

Second, consider schedules. Once your student has enrolled in a course, set weekly guidelines for course completion and establish a daily schedule to meet those goals. Jim Ryun, Olympic runner, said: "Motivation is what gets you started. Habit is what keeps you going."

Initially, be flexible, using the experience of the first few weeks to adjust time and effort up or down. If there are big problems with the course—too difficult, too easy, too boring, too bureaucratic—return it for a refund and try a different course.

Third, set the scene. Create a regular place to study, especially for traditional academic courses. This should include a well-stocked desk or computer work station. Isolate the work area from household interruptions and television.

Fourth, organize. I have been impressed more than once that people who got "A's" in college classes were not necessarily the smartest, but instead the best organized. Check out Appendix L, "Scoring A's In Traditional Courses".

Fifth, ask questions. Often instructors encourage interaction, only to have students ignore the opportunity. The sophisticated question-er tries to find answers in his course materials first. He looks up unknown words in glossaries and makes certain he understands assignments in the syllabus. If he cannot find answers, he asks the instructor immediately. He doesn't wait until the final examination. He carefully takes notes on the answer, and asks follow-up questions when answers are not clear.

Sixth, arrange for local, personal critiques. Any distance learner should create opportunities for local interpersonal feedback. Most homeschoolers begin with their parents. Be a sounding board. And help your student brainstorm solutions to problems presented by independent study. In addition, find another, more experienced independent study student to act as a mentor. And, if possible, find mentors who work in your teenager's target career field. That will give his studies more relevance, his education more depth, and his résumé more sparkle.

Chapter Highlights

- Distance Learning course offerings and programs are expanding rapidly.

- Homeschoolers consider college at home for individual courses, concurrent with high school, as well as for two-year and four-year degree programs after high school.

- Distance Learning is a great option for those who want to generate college credit with portfolios, test-outs, projects, and other demonstrations of non-traditional learning.

- College at home includes correspondence, telephone communications, TV and radio, e-mail, and the World Wide Web. Whether you have a computer or not, affordable options exist in most fields of study.

- Smart shopping techniques apply to college at home, just like everything else.

- Try a subject that plays to a student's strengths for his first college at home course. Plan and organize to maximize chances for success.

And What About College?

CHAPTER NINE

QUESTIONS AND ANSWERS

This book reflects the content of workshops and seminars I have conducted over the past eight years as well as e-mail critiques and correspondence resulting from the first edition. Here are answers to frequently asked questions.

Q: *Were your children really as productive every day as they appear in the cover letters?*

A: Of course not. Our teenagers had some very busy days, which we described in the cover letters. They also had days when they completely spaced out, days when they would literally lie outside on the grass and watch the clouds go by.

Two things kept our children from getting in prolonged slumps. First, daytime television was never an option, and we restricted nighttime television to an hour daily. In that situation, anyone will only stare at the four walls for so long. Second, my teenagers learned early that extended unproductive periods resulted in increased household chores.

Q: *How do we handle high school subjects in which we have no expertise?*

A: Sooner or later, every homeschool parent hits the wall—that is, encounters an unfamiliar subject. You have many options to explore when this happens:

- Find a self-instructional course. Locate these in large bookstores, college bookstores, and through independent study high schools and colleges. Mail order homeschooling suppliers also sell them.

The student works with the materials on his own, or the home-schooling parent learns with the student.

• Trade expertise with another homeschooling parent.

• Ask neighbors, friends, and relatives for help.

• Check with local hobbyists' groups. Study electronics with amateur radio operators, aerospace and aviation with flying clubs, speech and debate with Toastmasters, and so on.

• Find a volunteer opportunity that lets the student explore the subject. Backstage work with a community drama group applies.

• Take a class with the local high school, community college, adult education program, parks and recreation department, or YMCA.

• Consider accessing the information and expertise through community groups oriented towards youth: Civil Air Patrol, 4-H, Scouts, YMCA, church youth groups, and others.

• Pay a tutor or take private lessons. Local colleges and universities often can refer you to inexpensive college-age tutors.

Q: *Is it too late to begin homeschooling our tenth grade daughter?*

A: No. It is never too late to begin. I have known many students who began homeschooling in grades nine, ten, eleven, and twelve. These teenagers completed their high school studies in home-based programs and went on to college, apprenticeships, and paying jobs.

An interesting example is one eleventh grader who left high school. Having flunked almost everything in school, she had only completed three credits at age sixteen. As a homeschooler, she enrolled with American School, an independent study institution in

Illinois, and finished high school six months ahead of her former classmates.

Q: *Foreign language instruction seems impossible. Do you have any suggestions?*

A: The ideal way to learn a foreign language is to use it every day in real world contexts—in other words, to live in the country where it is spoken. Educators call instructional techniques that approach this situation "total immersion." Examples include watching a movie or following a recipe in the foreign language. Total immersion also usually involves listening and speaking before reading and writing.

Anything you do at home that approximates total immersion will help your student learn a foreign language. Unlike the situation with some other subjects, youth is an asset. Therefore, begin foreign language instruction as young as possible: elementary school age, if not younger. Use resources that emphasize listening before speaking, and listening and speaking before reading and writing. The goal is to hear the language for as much of the day as possible. Vocal music in the foreign language makes an indelible impression.

To begin foreign language study with a high school student, choose a language with which you have some experience. If you have no foreign language background, choose Spanish. Pronunciation is straightforward, and materials are readily available. Many home educators say Latin is also a good choice. Pronunciation is not critical, and excellent self-instructional materials exist for homeschoolers.

Resources that encourage total immersion include *The Learnables* (tapes in various languages), *Destinos* (a Spanish-language PBS instructional program), *Artes Latinae,* and *Learn To Speak Spanish* (or French) CD ROM from The Learning Company, and *The Rosetta Stone,* another CD ROM program. Often local colleges and universities have foreign language clubs that welcome teenage homeschoolers.

Unlike other subjects, foreign language might actually take longer at home than in public school. Begin not later than grade nine. Allow plenty of time to attain competency equivalent to two years of study, the minimum required by selective colleges. If the parents have no foreign language background, consider having the student take a high school or junior college class. Or hire or trade expertise with a fluent tutor.

Q: *My ninth-grade son just left school, where he was failing. He does not want to do anything, least of all school work. He also says he is not interested in anything. Help!*

A: He has just left a situation where he felt inept and stupid. He associates texts and exams and worksheets with failure. School probably also sent the message that his nonacademic interests were unimportant. Additionally, for the last nine to ten years, he has had most of his day scheduled for him. The net result—he is shell-shocked.

He will come out of it, but not overnight. Like it or not, he will spend the next six to twenty-four months going through something I call decompression. He needs time to get school out of his system. He needs time to discover what he knew at age five but what many schools destroy: that learning is fun. He also needs time to determine what he likes, what his interests are.

It is unrealistic to think that he will immediately become the model student just because you are homeschooling. With a decompressing student, try the following:

• Do not fill up all his time with academics. Been there, done that. It did not work.

• Allow plenty of alone time.

• Support any interests he displays. Examples are auto repair, computer programming, discussing the daily news, playing a musical instrument, drawing.

• Insist that he do a full complement of household chores daily.

- Get him to do things he has never tried before. Planning and cooking a meal or changing the oil in the car, for example. You can call this school.

- Encourage him to consider a volunteer job. Check out hospitals, libraries, drama groups, political campaigns, museums, and zoos. Again, call this school.

- Respect his choices of reading, and leave lots of interesting stuff lying around the house.

- Limit TV and mindless video games.

- Jointly choose a course of action for high school, whether that be a correspondence school or a family-devised program. Involve the student in all decisions.

In any case, read Grace Llewellyn's *Real Lives: Eleven Teenagers Who Don't Go To School.* Among the eleven essays are encouraging stories from students who left school and survived decompression to become self-directed learners.

Q: *Is it important to have a computer?*

A: Definitely. While it is not essential, it is very helpful. As retail prices decrease and computer hobbyists unload yesterday's hardware, new and used computers are moving into everyone's price range. Fortunately, most libraries now include word processor and Internet access in their services. Even those families with severe budgetary constraints can avail themselves of this resource to conduct research on the World Wide Web.

Do not be intimidated if you are computer-illiterate. As John Taylor Gatto, New York State Teacher of the Year and homeschool advocate, points out, most people in the United States were computer-illiterate 30 years ago, and many people who use computers today taught themselves.

Just as with foreign language study, computer literacy comes easiest to youngsters. Most likely, your children will teach themselves first and then ease your transition into computers and into cyberspace, the information superhighway. When I wrote our teenagers' transcripts, Jeff and Tamara put the finishing touches on those documents because they were further along the computer literacy learning curve than I was.

Consider other excellent reasons to acquire a computer. More and more courses are being offered via e-mail (electronic mail). independent study schools, at high school and college levels, teach their students via modem and computer. Major on-line services like America On-Line offer discussion groups dealing with homeschooling teenagers and with college admissions. Newest players in the homeschool discussion group scene are several excellent Internet-based discussion boards (see Appendix J). CD-ROM technology puts fun, interactive instructional materials at your fingertips.

Q: *Can homeschoolers win sports scholarships to college?*

A: Certainly. In our case, our son was actively recruited by the diving coach at West Point after working out with a Parks and Recreation Department competitive diving team for more than two years. Sports popular with home educators include gymnastics, martial arts, fencing, golf, tennis, soccer, swimming, and distance running. Many sports that earn college scholarship offers are available in your community through organizations like Police Athletic League, Parks and Recreation, the YMCA, adult-education classes, and local leagues and clubs. Check with local private clubs for certain sports and with private schools for others. Private schools often welcome homeschooler participation, for which they may charge a fee. In large metropolitan areas, you may even find several sports offered as activities through homeschool support groups.

In some states, homeschoolers can participate in public high school sports.

Certainly check to see what restrictions, if any, apply. Also, local community colleges may offer opportunities to play on their teams. If you pursue this tack, be certain that you understand your student's NCAA status See "The NCAA Guide for the College-bound Student Athelete," at www.ncaa.org/eligibility/cbsa and "Initial-Eligibility Procedures for Home-Schooled Student-Athletes," at www.ncaa.org/cbsa/home_school.html.

Q: *How do high school homeschoolers learn laboratory science?*

A: Science is all around you—in the kitchen, the bathroom, the garage, the garden. With the proper instructional materials, you can accomplish most high school laboratory science with things you have around the house. These instructional materials include books by Janice Van Cleave (*Experiments In Chemistry, Experiments In Biology*) and the Doubleday Made Simple series (*Chemistry Made Simple, Physics Made Simple*). Any large bookstore stocks these titles or will order them for you.

Castle Heights Press (800-763-7148) markets laboratory science manuals and kits for subjects like electronics, chemistry, and biology. The materials are challenging, teen-tested, hands-on, easy to use, and reasonably priced. I also like the interactive CD-ROM's like *Stars and Stories* (which includes hands-on projects) from Wildridge Software (888-244-4379).

Some independent study schools offer laboratory science courses, such as biology and chemistry. They send all the materials you need with the course. Alternatively, many high school homeschoolers enroll in junior college laboratory science courses during their high school years. Our son Jeff took geology at Community College of Aurora and physics at University of Denver.

Q: *Can we record Geometry taken in the 8th grade as 9th grade work?*

A: You, the homeschooling parent, are the principal, counselor, and teacher of a small private school. Like a small private school, you grant credit any way you want. Geometry at many schools is a high school level course. Most colleges will not question granting high school credit for it, regardless of the completion date. In short, use your common sense. If something seems comparable to high school level work, do not worry about the timing.

Q: *What is high school level work?*

A: Judging by the courses for which public high schools grant credit, high school level work is anything from remedial reading through calculus. We developed our criteria for our homeschool specifically to fit our educational philosophy and to satisfy our standards.

To qualify as a high school subject, our teenagers simply had to work on the topic for at least 60 hours (1/2 credit) and demonstrate that they had advanced their understanding of the subject.

Some home educators ignore time spent and instead apply a difficulty criterion. If the material covered is at least as challenging as a comparable high school text (again, there could be a lot of latitude here), they give credit.

Q. *How do we grant Advanced Placement (AP) credit?*

A. Just indicate the initials AP after the transcript course listing. An Advanced Placement course typically is a college-level study of English, American History, Biology, and so on. Course content should parallel that found in the AP study guides for various subjects, available in any large bookstore.

Students need not take the AP test for you to call a course Advanced Placement. The object of an AP course is a score of four or five out of five on the corresponding Advanced Placement test. Because admissions officers at selective colleges need unbiased performance evaluations of homeschoolers, generally homeschooled applicants to Ivy League and similar schools will want to followup and take the test.

The Pennsylvania Homeschoolers' Association has recently made Advanced Placement courses available to homeschoolers nationwide. For more information, contact:

Pennsylvania Homeschoolers, RR 2 Box 117, Kittanning, Pennsylvania 16201 or on-line at the Pennsylvania Homeschoolers' website: www.pahomeschoolers.com/courses/.

Q: *Do we have to include subjects on the transcript that the student did not complete?*

A: Again, you are the boss. We did not include dead-ends. To do so would have discouraged our children from experimenting with new topics. The teenage years are a time to explore, not a time to be penalized for exploring new subjects. Yes, both our son and daughter began projects and activities they never completed. Homeschooling, as efficient as it is, left plenty of time for both successful and incomplete ventures. We had more than enough material for the transcripts. No admissions officer questioned us about this. Do whatever you want. Just be consistent. If asked, be honest about your approach.

Q: *How did you assign grades?*

A: Schools use grades as a sorting mechanism and as reward or punishment, only secondarily as a rating of quality of work. Our approach was different. Our teenagers independently pursued many of the courses listed on our homeschool transcripts. Why? They were enthusiastic about the material. They did "A" work in those areas because of that enthusiasm.

With respect to the more traditional courses, we adopted the policy of sticking with it and reviewing if necessary until the student mastered the material. We did not compute grades for these more formal subjects. If the student completed the course at the mastery level, we usually figured that was worth an "A" on the transcript.

Others compute grades. They figure percentages of worksheets, tests, and papers; and they average those percentages for a final grade. They adopt a grading scale to assign a letter grade. One grading scale is 91-100%=A; 81-90%=B, and so on.

Q: *We plan to enroll our homeschooled teenager in an independent study program. We really don't need to write a transcript in addition to the external transcript, do we?*

A: No, you need not do a home-brew transcript. Homeschoolers have succeeded with college admissions using just external transcripts and filling out the forms as best they can. However, most students will be more competitive with either a home-brew transcript or portfolio—in addition to the transcript from the independent study program. A homeschool transcript includes subjects for which most independent study schools will not give credit. Examples are home economics, art, and consumer math. Certainly a master transcript is easier to read and evaluate than transcripts from multiple sources.

Q: *If we use an independent study high school, should it be accredited?*

A: As far as most colleges are concerned, high school accreditation for home educated students is a moot point. Our experience and that of hundreds of other homeschooling families indicates that while documentation and standardized test results are important, accreditation of the high school is not.

Public high schools do care, though. If your homeschooled student plans to return to high school, discuss credit for high school homeschooling with the high school counselors. Most likely, they will accept credits from other accredited schools. Get any commitment they make to accept homeschool credit in writing.

Keep in mind that the word accreditation means different things. Regional accreditation applies primarily to colleges and universities. Most government and private high schools have state accreditation. Correspondence and independent study schools generally seek accreditation from specialty distance-learning accrediting agencies. Colleges are open to just about anything from homeschoolers. High schools, illogically, are more picky. With respect to transferring units, many high schools will not find the different types of accreditation equally acceptable.

Q: *What about a diploma?*

A: Contrary to popular belief, a high school diploma is not a prerequisite for admission to most colleges and universities. Harvard's catalog specifically states that a high school diploma is not required. Looked at another way, the student only needs a high school diploma if he attended a government or private high school full time. Obviously, full-time high school attendance that does not result in a diploma is open to question.

As a homeschool principal, you can issue your own diploma. That allows your student to check the "yes" box whenever he is asked if he has a high school diploma on a job or college application. I find the wording on applications interesting. "Do you have a high school diploma?" is the usual form of the question. Seldom do applications say, "Do you have a high school diploma from an accredited school?"

If this issue greatly concerns you (although from a college application viewpoint, it need not), enroll the student in an accredited independent study or umbrella school that grants diplomas. Alternatively, the student can take the GED test to qualify for a general equivalency diploma.

Q: *Should our student take the GED?*

A: The GED or General Education Development test is a high school diploma granted to students who attain a minimum score on the GED test. The GED test is not difficult. Most 9th to 12th graders with average reading and math skills pass it. Any large bookstore carries GED study guides. Call local adult education programs, community colleges, and libraries for specific registration information.

Some colleges and universities may admit a homeschooler contingent on the student taking the GED "to complete their records." Some financial aid programs also require either a diploma or a GED score. No big deal. Just have the student sign up for and take the test. In some states, you may encounter problems because of the student's age because a few states do not allow individuals under age 19 to take the test. If this happens, inquire about an age waiver. Also, let the college which has provisionally admitted your student know about the problem. They may decide to waive the test.

Otherwise, for homeschoolers who will go to college, I see no point in taking the GED. Why will the student need a diploma of any kind if he has a bachelor's degree?

You will want to think most carefully about taking the GED if the your student plans to enlist in the armed forces. Traditionally, the military has put GED holders on a lower tier of acceptance than students with high school diplomas. That's the bad news.

The good news is that the Air Force has recently revised its policies with respect to homeschoolers. They created a separate 2% recruiting category for homeschooled students, far in excess of the current numbers. Regulations for homeschoolers pursuing military enlistment are in a state of flux. Check with local recruiters for updates.

If you think your teen will enlist in the military, consider enrolling him in a regionally or state-accredited diploma-granting correspondence school for high school. Or make sure the student completes at least 16 college credits during high school. Those with a GED and 16 college credits go right back in the selection hopper with the diploma holders.

Q: *What about graduating early?*

A: Many homeschooled teenagers do complete their high school studies ahead of schedule, not because homeschoolers are smarter than everyone else but because homeschooling itself is so efficient. The question then becomes what to do with fifteen-, sixteen-, and seventeen-year-olds who are ready to move on.

Sending the student to college early is one choice, but it is an option that should be carefully evaluated. Weigh the pros and cons. Many intellectually sophisticated 16-year olds are not ready for the social pressures, even those of very conservative colleges. Many 40-year-olds would not be ready for some of the pressures!

Option number two. As discussed in the previous chapter, integrate some college work into the high school homeschooling program. Students take community college classes or independent study college courses concurrent with their high school homeschooling.

Third choice. Those who have finished high school can enroll full time in an independent study program for college. They may finish two to four years of college at home prior to age 18. See John Bear's *Guide To Non-Traditional College Degrees* and Alexandra Swann's book, *No Regrets: How Homeschooling Earned Me A Master's Degree At Age 16.*

Lastly, consider allowing the student more time during his high school years to pursue his interests in depth. This could involve travel, work, and special projects. Our 16-year-old daughter Tamara spent nine months in Australia, living with a host family, attending school, and working. For more ideas, read Grace Llewellyn's *The Teenage Liberation Handbook.*

Q: *Is college credit earned in high school transferable? Will the college our student eventually attends recognize the credit?*

A: The answer here is maybe. Each college determines which previously taken college classes are transferable. If you have an idea where your student might end up, query that college ahead of time. None of our son Jeff's college credits transferred to the Air Force Academy. He and all the other students there began with a blank slate.

There is little doubt, though, that taking the college classes as part of his high school homeschooling helped him win the Academy appointments. The background probably also won him the ROTC scholarship offers. Most importantly, the college courses prepared him for the academic rigors of a selective school.

Q: *How much responsibility should the student take for the college application?*

A: All of it. Your homeschooler should make calls to obtain applications, ask for letters of recommendation, keep track of deadlines, complete standardized test registrations, and so on. Some teenagers will not do the leg work. Those lacking motivation should consider delaying college and consider alternatives like the military and full-time and volunteer work. In the application process, parents ideally function most of the time as facilitators, ready with encouragement, ideas, wheels, and financing.

Q: *Should our teen discuss home education as the essay topic?*

A: There are increasing numbers of homeschooled students applying to colleges. Homeschooling as an application essay topic is likely to appear more often. If it hasn't happened already, it will soon lose its novelty.

The student should only discuss homeschooling as the essay topic in two situations. In the first instance, homeschooling is an area of particular interest and concern, above and beyond other activities and topics. In the second instance, the student has a unique slant on some aspect of home education.

Q: *Should we prepare our student for interviews?*

A: More good news here. Most colleges and universities do not require interviews. So, first, call the colleges of interest and determine if this is an issue. If it is, The Princeton Review *Student Access Guide to College Admissions* contains excellent interview guidelines.

Jeff had interviews with military academy, ROTC, and congressional representatives. He found, much to his frustration, that some of these interviewers were more interested in homeschooling than in his particular activities and accomplishments. He answered questions about the pros and cons of home education, when he would rather have been discussing his private pilot training.

Be aware that your students may find themselves in similar situations. Prepare them for interviews using the Princeton Review guidelines recommended above. Make certain they can answer questions about how and why you homeschool.

Q. *How much should our teenager emphasize ethnic and socio-economic background on his college applications?*

A. Michele Hernandez, in *A Is For Admission*, lists the following Ivy League "tip factors," student background that may tip a borderline applicant in the direction of admittance. These are legacies (mom or dad attended the same school), recruited athletes, blacks, Hispanics, and Native Americans. Interestingly, geographic diversity is not on her list. Neither do ethnic minorities like Chinese, Japanese, and so on make the cut. Certainly, if your son or daughter applies to a selective college or university, cite any tip factors that exist.

Ms. Hernandez also points out a subtle tip factor. First-generation college applicants, that is, students whose parents and grandparents did not graduate from college, as well as those low on the socioeconomic pecking order, are almost always given extra consideration. Consequently, she urges applicants from well-off families to be vague about that fact. And she encourages those from families that struggle to make ends meet to advertise that.

According to Ms. Hernandez, "We look at parents' information to get a general sense of background so we can see test scores in an appropriate context." It sounds like an 1150 SAT score may mean more from an "underprivileged" student than from an applicant who attended a fancy Ivy League prep school.

Q: *How are Jeff and Tamara doing?*

A: As I write this early in the year 2000, Jeff flies F-16's in Korea as a First Lieutenant in the U.S. Air Force. He graduated from the Air

Force Academy in 1997 with a degree in aeronautical engineering and made the academic honor roll every semester. At the academy, he flew for the competition flying team. Since graduating from college, he has spent more than two years in jet pilot training, consistently performing at the top of his class. He is now one of the youngest F-16 pilots in the Air Force.

Even though we see him only two to four weeks each year, we keep in close touch with almost daily e-mail and electronic chats. Jeff has no regrets about his decision to attend the academy and learning to fly jets. Just like other pilots, he often says, "I cannot believe they are paying me to do this."

Since completing her education at home, Tamara alternates college attendance with work. She has accumulated approximately three years of college credit from four different colleges. Not one has questioned her homeschool background. She has also held several jobs, including restaurant hostess, health club receptionist, health food store manager, caterer, and advertising sales assistant.

Tamara currently takes one college class and works full-time selling display advertising for a local newspaper in San Luis Obispo, California. She also teaches piano, throws pots, and occasionally writes for publication. She says she wants to get her degree eventually, but is in no hurry. Because she lives just twenty minutes north of our location, we see her several times each month.

Appendices

Appendix A—Transcripts and Homeschool Course Descriptions

Appendix B—Cover letters

Appendix C—Résumés

Appendix D—Application Essays

Appendix E—Sample Eclectic Curricula

Appendix F—Some Selective Colleges That Have Admitted Home-schooled Students

Appendix G—Colleges of Special Interest to Homeschoolers

Appendix H—A Few Pointers On Applying To A Service Academy

Appendix I—Homeschoolers' College Planning Checklist

Appendix J—Resources

Appencix K—After-The-Fact Curriculum

Appendix L—Scoring A's In Traditional Courses

Appendix A

Transcripts and Homeschool Course Descriptions

Here are copies of the transcripts we used for our children. They include course credits and descriptions, plus grades and grade point averages. I also included two pages of the originals so you can see how they can look—and be accepted by admissions offices—when you use a typewriter or word processor.

Desert-Mountain Homeschool High School (Grades 9-12)

Transcript (September, 1990 - January, 1993)

Jeffrey Scott Cohen   SSAN: _____
(Address)

Completed Courses	Grade	Credit	Date
Desert-Mountain Homeschool Courses:			
(Course descriptions attached)			
Algebra II	A	1	12/90
Advanced Mathmatics	A	2	12/91
(Geom/Trig/Alg III)			
Calculus (AP)	A	1	10/92
Radio Electronics	A	1	11/91
Aerospace/Aviation	A	1	07/91
Military Leadership I & II	A	1	07/92
Piano Performance I	A	1	05/91
Music Theory/Appreciation	A	1	05/91
PE: Diving I	A	1	05/91
Private Pilot Training	A	1/2	07/92
Aviation Challenge	A	1/2	06/92

Total Desert-Mountain Homeschool Credits 11

Completed Courses   Grade   Credit   Date

American School Courses:

Course	Grade	Credit	Date
Algebra I	A	1	01/91
Geometry	A	1	12/91
Biology I (laboratory)	A	1	06/91
Chemistry	A	1	12/91
Oceanography	A	1	03/92
US History	A	1	11/90
World History	A	1	10/91
Psychology	A	1	10/90
Social Civics	A	1	09/91
World Geography	A	1	05/91
Understanding English I	A	1	11/90
Understanding English II	A	1	09/91
English Grammar & Comp III	A	1/2	07/92
English Grammar & Comp IV	A	1/2	10/92
American Literature	A	1	07/92
English Literature	A	1	09/92
Spanish I	A	1	06/92

Total American School Credits: **16**

Total Carnegie Credits   **27**

Cumulative High School GPA: 4.0
(A=4.0,B=3.0,C=2.0,D=1.0)

Note: Carnegie Credit System: 1 unit of credit=120 hours
of study (American School and Desert-Mountain Homeschool award
1 Carnegie Credit for 120 or more hours of study).

Completed Courses

Community College of Aurora (Spring, 1992)

	Grade	Semester Hours
Geology 111: Physical Geology	A	4
Computer Sys 101:	A	2
Computer Sys 095: Laboratory	CR	1

University of Denver (Summer, 1992)

		Quarter Hrs
Engineering 50	B	4

University of Denver (Fall, 1992)

Mathematics 1950 (1) Calculus	A	4
University Physics 1210 (1)	B	4
University Physics Lab 1220 (1)	B+	1

In-Progress Courses (Winter/Spring, 1993)

Desert-Mountain Homeschool — Carnegie Credit

	Carnegie Credit
Etymology/Vocabulary	1
PE: Diving Team	1
Piano Performance	1
Private Pilot License	1

American School — Carnegie Credit

	Carnegie Credit
Spanish II	1

University of Denver (Winter, 1993)   **Quarter Hours**

Mathematics 1950 (2) Calculus	4
University Physics 1210 (2)	4
University Physics Laboratory 1220 (2)	1

University of Denver (Spring, 1993)

Mathematics 1950 (3) Calculus	4
University Physics 1210 (3)	4
University Physics 1220 (3)	1
Mathematics 1950 (2) Calculus	4
University Physics 1210 (2)	4
University Physics Laboratory 1220 (2)	1

University of Denver (Spring, 1993)

Mathematics 1950 (3) Calculus	4
University Physics 1210 (3	4
University Physics 1220 (3)	1

Desert-Mountain Homeschool High School

Course Descriptions

Student: Jeffrey Scott Cohen   SSAN: _____

Math

Algebra II: This course completes the automation of the fundamental skills of algebra. Content includes uniform motion problems; boat-in-the-river problems; systems of linear equations in two unknowns, in three unknowns plus systems of non-linear equations; area, volume, and unit conversions; right angle trigonometry; conversions of rectangular-to-polar and polar-to-rectangular coordinates and addition of vectors; similar triangles; complex numbers; completing the square; deriving and using the quadratic formula. Chemical mixture problems are addressed. Text: *Algebra II, An Incremental Development* by John Saxon. Course consists of 129 lessons and problem sets with a cumulative test given every fourth lesson.

Advanced Mathematics: This integrated two-year course is the culmination of the process of acquiring the fundamental skills of algebra, geometry, and trigonometry. Content includes a concentrated study of geometric proofs; logarithms; trigonometric identities; infinite series; conic sections; matrices and determinants; echelon solutions; abstract word problems. Text: *Advanced Mathematics (Geometry/Trigonometry/Algebra III), An Incremental Development* by John Saxon. Course is comprised of 119 lessons and problem sets, with a cumulative test given every fourth lesson.

Calculus: In-depth coverage of all topics required for the AB Advanced Placement calculus exam. Included is a thorough review of logarithmic and trigonometric functions. Other topics are mathematical proofs, maxima and minima applications, polar form of complex numbers. Core of course is single variable calculus and analytic geometry; limits, continuity, derivatives, applications of deriva-

128

tives, indefinite and definite integrals and their applications, calculus of transcendental functions, techniques of integration, calculus of polar coordinates, analytic geometry, improper integrals, and infinite review series. Text is Calculus with *Trigonometry and Analytic Geometry* by John Saxon and Frank Wang. 117 lessons and problem sets with a cumulative test every fourth lesson.

Science

Aerospace/Aviation Studies: This introduction to aerospace and aviation includes the following units:

• History of Air and Space Flight

• Aircraft and Their Uses

• Aerodynamics, Flight, and Propulsion

• Aerial Navigation and the Weather

• Space Exploration Today and Tomorrow

• The Aerospace Community
Text is: *Horizons Unlimited* published by National Headquarters Civil Air Patrol, Maxwell AFB, Alabama. Course consists of readings, videos, lectures.

Radio Electronics: Course consists of self-study of text materials and amateur radio operating practice needed to pass the FCC Advanced Class Amateur Radio Operator License Examination. Text is the *Advanced Class License Manual for the Radio Amateur.* Topics covered include radio wave propagation, amateur radio practice, electrical principles, circuit components, practical circuits, signals and emissions, antennas and feed lines. Successful completion of course consists of passing the FCC Advanced Class License Examination.

English

Etymology/Vocabulary: Based on the text, *English Words From Latin and Greek Elements,* by Donald M. Ayers, Revised by Thomas D. Worthen, and the accompanying workbook. Course covers the Indo-European family of languages and the development of English vocabulary, dictionary usage, Greek and Latin affixes and bases, and word analysis.

Music

Piano Performance I and II: Courses consist of weekly lessons and daily practice. At least four performances of at least two pieces are required per year. Participation in the American Guild of Piano Teachers auditions (with a ten-piece program) is required each spring.

Music Theory/Appreciation: Theory covers music fundamentals (notation, rhythm, scales, key signatures, intervals, chords), beginning diatonic harmony and analysis, and ear training. Appreciation covers the basic materials of music, musical forms, genres, musical periods, and composers.

Physical Education

PE: Diving I & II: Participation on APR Rippers Diving Team, a comprehensive US Diving Program including 5 hours practice weekly plus monthly diving meets. Also included is a personal conditioning program which consists of distance running and upper body strengthening.

Miscellaneous

Military Leadership Studies I and II: Military Customs and

Courtesies plus participation in Civil Air Patrol through the Mitchell Award (I) and the Earhart Award (II).

Aviation Challenge: Introduces the discipline and rigors of military pilot training. Includes simulator flights, water survival, classroom aeronautics and air crew procedures, aircraft carrier operations, field take-off and landing procedures, precision aerobatics in high performance jet simulators. Course conducted at US Space Academy, Huntsville, AL.

Private Pilot Training: Instruction up to and including the first solo flight through the Civil Air Patrol Colorado Wing Flight Encampment.

Private Pilot License: In-the-air pilot training plus text studies leading the FAA Private Pilot License.

Reproductions of two pages from Jeff's original transcript as submitted with his applications.

Desert-Mountain Homeschool High School (Grades 9-12) **Transcript**
    (September, 1990 - January, 1993)

Jeffery Scott Cohen   SSAN: _____
    (Address)

Completed Courses

	Grade	Credit	Date
Desert-Mountain Homeschool Courses:			
(Course descriptions attached)			
Algebra II — — — — — — — — — A	1	12/90
Advanced Mathmatics — — — — — A	2	12/91
(Geometry, Trigonometry, Algebra III)		
Calculus (Advanced Placement) A	1	10/92
Radio Electronics — — — — — — A	1	11/91
Aerospace/Aviation— — — — — — A	1	07/91
Military Leadership I & II— — A	1	07/92
Piano Performance I — — — — — A	1	05/91
Music Theory/Appreciation — — A	1	05/91
PE: Diving I — — — — — — — — A	1	05/91
Private Pilot Training— — — — A	1/2	07/92
Aviation Challenge— — — — — — A	1/2	06/92

Total Desert-Mountain Homeschool Credits 11

American School Courses:

Algebra I - - - - - - - - - - A	1	01/91
Geometry - - - - - - - - - - A	1	12/91
Biology I (laboratory)- - - - A	1	06/91
Chemistry - - - - - - - - - - A	1	12/91
Oceanography - - - - - - - - A	1	03/92
US History — — — — — — — — — A	1	11/90
World History — — — — — — — — A	1	10/91
Psychology — — — — — — — — — A	1	10/90
Social Civics — — — — — — — — A	1	09/91
World Geography — — — — — — — A	1	05/91
Understanding English I — — — A	1	11/90
Understanding English II— — — A	1	09/91
English Grammar & Comp III— — A	1/2	07/92
English Grammar & Comp IV — — A	1/2	10/92
American Literature — — — — — A	1	07/92
English Literature— — — — — — A	1	09/92
Spanish I — — — — — — — — — — A	1	06/92

Total American School Credits: 16

TRANSCRIPT: Jeffrey S. Cohen   P. 2

COMPLETED COURSES (Con't.)

Total Carnegie Credits   27

Cumulative High School GPA: 4.0 (A=4.0,B=3.0,C=2.0,D=1.0)

Note: Carnegie Credit System: 1 unit of credit = 120 hours
of study (American School and Desert-Mountain Homeschool
award 1 Carnegie Credit for 120 or more hours of study).

Community College of Aurora courses
(Spring, 1992)

		Grade	Semester
Geology 111:	Physical Geology — — — — — A		4
Computer Sys 101:	MS-DOS/PC-DOS — — — — A		2
Computer Sys 095:	Laboratory — — — — — CR		1

University of Denver (Summer, 1992)   Quarter hours
Engineering 50— — — — — — — — — — — — — B   4

University of Denver (Fall, 1992)
Mathematics 1950 (1) Calculus — — — — — — A	4
University Physics 1210 (1) — — — — — — — B	4
University Physics Lab 1220 (1) — — — B+	1

In-ProgressCourses (Winter/Spring, 1993)

Desert-Mountain Homeschool   Carnegie Credit
Etymology/Vocabulary	1
PE: Diving Team	1
Piano Performance	1
Private Pilot License	1

American School
Spanish II   1

University of Denver (Winter, 1993)   Quarter Hours
Mathematics 1950 (2) Calculus	4
University Physics 1210 (2)	4
University Physics Laboratory 1220 (2)	1

University of Denver (Spring, 1993)
Mathematics 1950 (3) Calculus	4
University Physics 1210 (3	4
University Physics 1220 (3)	1

Desert-Mountain Homeschool High School Transcript

Tamara Gail Cohen   SSAN: _____
(Address)

Homeschool Courses (Course descriptions attached)

Course:	Grade*	Credit**	Date
Advanced Mathematics (AP)	A	1	12/92
Spanish I	A	1	01/94
World Geography	A	1	12/91
Contemporary Authors	A	1	06/91
English Vocabulary	A	1	06/91
Latin I	A	1	12/92
Bible Studies	A	1	12/92
Physical Education: Tae Kwon Do	A	1	12/92
Physical Education: Lifetime Sports	A	1	06/92
Physical Education: Netball	A	1	09/94
Introduction to Computers	A	1/2	12/94

Total Desert-Mountain Home School Credits: 10 1/2

*"Credit" calculated according to Carnegie credit standard = 120 or more contact hours
**"Grades" awarded according to a numerical grading schedule:
    A = 93% to 100%   D = 65% to 75%
    B = 85% to 92%   F = below 65%
    C = 76% to 84%
    "Pass/Fail Courses" are indicated as follows: P = Pass   F = Fail

Desert-Mountain Homeschool High School Transcript

Tamara Gail Cohen   SSAN: _____
(Address)

American School Courses

Course:	Grade*	Credit**	Date
Algebra I	A	1	07/92
Geometry	A	1	11/92
Algebra II and Trigonometry	A	1	04/93
Biology I (with Laboratory)	A	1	10/92
Ecology	A	1	10/93
Physiology and Health	A	1	10/93
US History	A	1	06/92
World History	A	1	04/93
Civics/Government	A	1	12/92
English Grammar & Composition I	B	1/2	12/92
English Grammar & Composition II	A	1/2	01/93
English Grammar & Composition III	A	1/2	07/93
English Grammar & Composition IV	A	1/2	12/93
American Literature	B	1	06/93
English Literature	A	1	08/93
Careers	A	1	01/93
Psychology	A	1	06/92
Clothing Construction	A	1	06/92

Total American School Credits: **16**

American School High School Diploma Granted   28 Feb 1994

*"Credit" calculated according to Carnegie credit standard = 120 or more contact hours
**"Grades" awarded according to a numerical grading schedule:

      A = 93% to 100%   D = 65% to 75%
      B = 85% to 92%   F = below 65%
      C = 76% to 84%
      "Pass/Fail Courses" are indicated as follows: P = Pass   F = Fail

Desert-Mountain Homeschool High School Transcript

Tamara Gail Cohen   SSAN: _____
(Address)

Overland High School Courses
(Cherry Creek School District, Aurora, Colorado)

Course:	Grade*	Credit**	Date
Trebelaires (Women's Choir)	A	1/2	12/91
Trebelaires	A	1/2	06/92
Voice Performance	A	1/2	12/91
Trebelaires	A	1/2	12/92
Trebelaires	A	1/2	06/93
Drama I	A	1/2	12/92

Total Overland High School Credits: 3

Bendigo, Australia Senior Secondary High School
(Course descriptions attached)

Course:	Grade*	Credit**	Date
English	P	1	10/94
Math	P	1	10/94
Geography	P	1/2	10/94
Drama	P	1	10/94

Total Australian Secondary High School Credits: **3 1/2**

Total Completed Carnegie Credits: **33**

Cumulative High School GPA: 3.95
    (A=4.0   B=3.0   C=2.0   D=1.0)

Desert-Mountain Homeschool High School Transcript

Tamara Gail Cohen   SSAN: _____
(Address)

In-Progress Courses

Desert-Mountain Homeschool Courses (Fall 1994)   Credits**

Spanish II	1
Physics (AP) with Laboratory	1

	College
Wright State University Courses	**Qtr Hrs**

Winter Quarter 1995

Communications 101: Essentials of Public Address	3
English 101: Freshman Composition	4

Spring Quarter 1995

Communications 102: Essentials of Interpersonal Communication	
	3
English 102: Freshman Composition	4

*"Credit" calculated according to Carnegie credit standard = 120 or more contact hours
**"Grades" awarded according to a numerical grading schedule:
    A = 93% to 100%   D = 65% to 75%
    B = 85% to 92%   F = below 65%
    C = 76% to 84%
    "Pass/Fail Courses" are indicated as follows: P = Pass   F = Fail

Desert-Mountain Homeschool High School

Course Descriptions

Student: Tamara Gail Cohen   SSAN: _____

Advanced Mathematics (AP): Culmination of the process of acquiring fundamental skills of algebra, geometry, and trigonometry. Content includes a concentrated study of geometric proofs; logarithms, trigonometric identities, infinite series, conic sections, matrices and determinants, echelon solutions; abstract word problems. Text: *Advanced Mathematics, An Incremental Development* by John Saxon (1 credit).

Latin I: First year Latin course, covering vocabulary, grammar, translation, Latin phrases used in English, and Roman history and culture. Materials include *Preparatory Latin, Book I*, 2nd Ed. by Buehner and Ambrose, *College Latin* by DeWitt, Gummere, and Horn, *Pompeiiana Newsletter*, plus *Artes Latinae* and *Language 30 Latin Tapes* (1 credit).

Spanish I: Basic conversational Spanish is emphasized in this introductory course. Through extensive listening and speaking practice and by reading children's books in Spanish, student learns basic sentence structure, parts of speech, and regular and irregular verbs in the present tense. Vocabulary development includes clothing, the house, time, weather, the calendar, numbers, and family relationships. Geography of the Spanish-speaking world is reviewed (1 credit).

Spanish II: Through such diverse topics as history of Spanish-speaking countries and traditional Hispanic foods, student increases vocabulary. Conversational Spanish continues to be emphasized together with an increase in the student's ability to read and write Spanish. Focus is on the study of stem-changing and irregular verbs, possessive adjectives, comparison of adjectives, and the preterite tense. Cultures of Spanish-speaking countries are examined (1 credit).

World Geography: Course consists of an overview of physical, political, and economic geography. Topics include the resources and needs of the world's nations the relationship between people and the land they live on, the kinds of land forms and climates that form our physical environment, how people are distributed over the earth, how they make their living from it, and how they change it. Materials include the game, *Where In The World*, National Geographic videos, atlases, and articles from *National Geographic* magazine and daily newspapers (1 credit).

Contemporary Authors: An introduction to 20th-century authors based on student-selected readings and subsequent discussions. Forms are the short story, novel, biography, poetry, works in translation, and newspaper and magazine articles. Selections include: *A Separate Peace; Gone With The Wind; The Best of Roald Dahl* (short stories); *Robert Frost* (poetry); *Alicia: My Story; East of Eden; Lost Horizon; The Diary of Anne Frank* (1 credit).

English Vocabulary: Based on the text, *English Words from Greek and Latin Elements* by Donald M. Ayers, Revised by Thomas D. Worthen, and the accompanying workbook. Course covers the Indo-European family of languages and the development of English vocabulary, dictionary usage, Greek and Latin affixes/bases, and word analysis (1 credit).

Bible Studies: Bible readings from the *Living Bible*, including Genesis, Exodus, Job, Psalms, Ecclesiastes, and the entire New Testament plus discussion and group activities related to the readings (1 credit).

Physical Education: Tae Kwon Do: Elementary and mid-level kicks, elementary & advanced punching, blocking skills, take-down maneuvers, patterns, Korean terminology, relaxation focusing skills, self-defense (1 credit).

Physical Education: Lifetime Sports and Fitness: Cycling, running, walking, hiking, and cross-country skiing as a means to promote lifetime fitness are explored. Also included are nutritional studies

and meal planning to enhance lifetime fitness (1 credit).
Physical Education: Netball: Games 3 hours weekly. Skill development included passing, shooting, scoring, running, umpiring, strategy, and working together as a team (1 credit)

Introduction To Computers: Hands-on experience with student's own IBM-clone 386-PC. Commands, directories and subdirectories, file management and printing, Basic word processing using WordPerfect 5.1: opening, formatting, saving, and printing files; using graphics, fonts, and layout. Keyboarding basics and practice (1/2 credit).

Physics (AP) and Lab: Lessons include Newton's laws, statics, dynamics, thermodynamics, optics, dc circuits, waves, electromagnetics, and special relativity. Simple experiments and demonstrations relate physical concepts to everyday life. Two in-depth laboratory units – on electronics and optics – allow student to gain hands-on experience with real world applications. Text is *Physics: An Incremental Approach* by John Saxon; lab manuals are *Experiments in Physics* by Janice Van Cleave and *First Steps In Electronics* by Kathleen Julicher (1 credit).

Course Descriptions

Bendigo Senior Secondary School/Australia

[Note: Because we could not obtain copies of the course descriptions from Australia, these course descriptions were written by Tamara Cohen, after returning to the US. Because of the way the exchange program was set up, Tamara missed the first two weeks and the last two weeks of the school year, which ran from January through October. Classroom time included more than 120 hours for each 1 credit course, 60 hours for the 1/2 credit course.]

Maths/Statistics: Course included a detailed look at statistics and probability. Practical problem solving was emphasized. One work requirement was an essay of 1500 words on the movement of tides and the calculating probability of their height at different times. Computer simulations of various topics (efficiency studies, probability problems) involved using a spreadsheet and random number generator (1 credit).

English: Course included both writing skills and English Literature. Use of imagery in four works was closely studied: *The Kitchen God's Wife, The Crucible* (including a field trip to see a production), *The Third Man,* and *The Paper Nautilus.* Persuasive, creative, descriptive, and instructional writing were all practiced. An essay of 2000 words on a current and controversial topic was a work requirement (1 credit).

Drama: In-depth review of the dramatic arts both modern and classical works. Two plays, Shakespeare's *Romeo and Juliet* and *Cosi* (an Australian play) were closely studied. Both group and solo performances were mandatory and graded. Special attention was given to the methods of Shakespeare and other classical playwrights. Class included attendance at an acting workshop in Melbourne (1 credit).

Geography: Course focused on Australian physical, political, historical, and economic geography. Topics included government influences on Australian land use and how Australian geography influenced development of the country. Students completed a field trip to the Melbourne Museum of Natural History and hands-on geographic studies (measuring rainfall, studying soil samples) (1/2 credit).

Reading List (1994–1995)

I Know Why The Caged Bird Sings (Maya Angelou)

Lord of The Flies (William Golding)

Princess (Jean P. Sassoon)

Bess W. Truman (Margaret Truman)

To Kill A Mockingbird (Harper Lee)

Going Solo (Roald Dahl)

Queen (Alex Haley)

The Grapes of Wrath (John Steinbeck)

Alice's Adventures in Wonderland (Lewis Carroll)

Animal Farm (George Orwell)

This Boy's Life (Tobias Wolff)

Bible, New International Version (Proverbs and New Testament Selections)

Maus I and *Maus II* (Art Spiegelman)

Much Ado About Nothing (William Shakespeare)

As You Like It (William Shakespeare)

The Raven and other poems (Poe)

When Heaven and Earth Changed Places (Le Ly Hayslip)

It Was On Fire When I Lay Down On It (Robert Fulghum)

Reproductions of two pages from Tamara's original transcript as submitted with her applications.

Desert-Mountain Homeschool High School

Transcript

Student: TAMARA GAIL COHEN *SSAN:* _____ *Date of Birth:*

Issued to: (College Admissions address)   Date of Issue: Dec. 11, 1994

Homeschool Courses (Course descriptions attached)

Course:	Grade*	Credit**	Date
Advanced Mathematics (AP)	A	1	12/92
Spanish I	A	1	01/94
World Geography	A	1	12/91
Contemporary Authors	A	1	06/91
English Vocabulary	A	1	06/91
Latin I	A	1	12/92
Bible Studies	A	1	12/92
Physical Education: Tae Kwon Do	A	1	12/92
Physical Education: Lifetime Sports	A	1	06/92
Physical Education: Netball	A	1	09/94
Introduction to Computers	A	1/2	12/94

Total Desert-Mountain Home School Credits: 10 1/2

---

*"Credit" calculated according to Carnegie credit standard = 120 or more contact hours
**"Grades" awarded according to a numerical grading schedule:

    A = 93% to 100%   D = 65% to 75%
    B = 85% to 92%   F = below 65%
    C = 76% to 84%
    "Pass/Fail Courses" are indicated as follows: P = Pass   F = Fail

Desert-Mountain Homeschool High School

Transcript

Student: TAMARA GAIL COHEN *SSAN:* _____ *Date of Birth:*

Issued to: (College Admissions address)   Date of Issue: Dec. 11, 1994

Overland High School Courses

(Cherry Creek School District, Aurora, Colorado)

Course:	Grade*	Credit**	Date
Trebelaires (Women's Choir)	A	1/2	12/91
Trebelaires	A	1/2	06/92
Voice Performance	A	1/2	12/91
Trebelaires	A	1/2	12/92
Trebelaires	A	1/2	06/93
Drama I	A	1/2	12/92
Total Overland High School Credits:		3	

Bendigo, Australia Senior Secondary High School

(Course descriptions attached)

Course:	Grade*	Credit**	Date
English	P	1	10/94
Math	P	1	10/94
Geography	P	1/2	10/94
Drama	P	1	10/94
Total Australian Secondary High School Credits:		3 1/2	

Total Completed Carnegie Credits: 33

Cumulative High School GPA: 3.95 (A=4.0 B=3.0 C=2.0 D=1.0)

---

*"Credit" calculated according to Carnegie credit standard = 120 or more contact hours
**"Grades" awarded according to a numerical grading schedule:
    A = 93% to 100%   D = 65% to 75%
    B = 85% to 92%   F = below 65%
    C = 76% to 84%
    "Pass/Fail Courses" are indicated as follows: P = Pass   F = Fail

TWO COVER LETTERS

Here are two of the cover letters I wrote for my son's and daughter's college applications. These letters were customized to address questions these schools asked on their counselor recommendation forms.

Desert-Mountain Homeschool   10 January 1993
[Address]
Admissions Records
Boston University
[Address]
Re: Teacher Recommendation, High School Report, and Mid-Year Report for Jeffrey Scott Cohen, [Social Security Number]

Sirs:

Jeffrey Cohen is a high school senior in our home-based education program. I, his parent and principal facilitator ("teacher" would be an inappropriate designation), am writing this letter in lieu of completing the Teacher Recommendation, High School Counselor Recommendations, and Mid-year School Report. Jeff's current college instructors at University of Denver have told us they do not complete these types of forms for any student.

Although Jeff has a high school diploma from an independent-study high school, American School, we will consider him graduated when he completes the requirements of Desert-Mountain Homeschool, including college courses in which he is presently enrolled. By April, 1993, Jeff will not only have completed high school in three years (rather than four), he also will have accumulated the equivalent of at least 20 college semester units at Community

College of Aurora and at University of Denver. We consider these college credits to be a part of Jeff's high school program.

About half of Jeff's high school work has been accomplished through Amercian School, a fully accredited independent-study institution in Chicago, IL. We have supplemented American School studies with our own courses, including *Saxon Mathematics* through Calculus and Analytic Geometry, aerospace studies and military leadership training with Civil Air Patrol, a vocabulary course, music courses, and physical education (diving team and personal conditioning). Jeff devised his own course of study and taught himself radio electronics to pass the FCC Advanced Class Amateur Radio Operator test. We've also counted Jeff's work towards his private pilot's license as part of his high school curriculum.

This information is summarized on the two-page Desert-Mountain Homeschool Transcript enclosed. With that are copies of the transcript from American School, Community College of Aurora, and University of Denver. Official transcripts are also being sent directly from these institutions. Also enclosed is a current schedule from the University of Denver showing Jeff's in-progress classes (Physics and Calculus).

Our homeschooling is best characterized by the word "eclectic." Jeff and I jointly establish learning goals and try to locate the best resources in or out of traditional school settings to accomplish those goals.

A sample day in our home-based program best serves to illustrate Jeff's motivation, intellectual qualities, academic achievement, and potential for growth. Last Tuesday, Jeff got up and ran three miles. This is part of his self-devised physical training program. After breakfast, Jeff practiced piano for an hour. He is preparing advanced recital material (Bach Prelude and Fugue and Mozart Sonata) for the spring. He then drove to University of Denver and attended two classes, Calculus and Physics Laboratory. After class, he stopped by a music store to pick up material for one of his piano students. He's been teaching piano for two years. His students have included adults and children.

Jeff returned home and worked on Spanish, one of his independent-study courses from American School. He made several calls to schedule an airplane for his next flying lesson. In the afternoon, he went to diving practice. He spent the evening at home studying and preparing a rocketry course he's teaching for his Civil Air Patrol squadron. He also volunteered about one hour to the Military Affiliate Radio System (MARS). He's an FCC-licensed Amateur Radio Operator and enjoys helping servicemen overseas communicate with their families here.

Jeff juggles a number of activities, and the line between the academic and non-academic becomes fuzzy at times. Our emphasis has been on self-directed learning, on learing how to learn, including learning to take advantage of a wide range of community resources. We think of our home school as a place where we are all learning all the time.

In his life organization skills and in his conduct with others, Jeff displays a high level of maturity. He successfully schedules and keeps up with a wide range of activities (see attached résumé). He recognizes all individuals, regardless of age, as peers, as potential teachers. As the leader of his Civil Air Patrol squadron, he successfully initiated and carried out many activities with his age mates, including a wilderness survival weekend, a model rocketry course, and several recruiting drives. He recognizes the importance of devoting time to church and volunteer activities.

Jeff's strengths include his organizational skills and his adoption of the self-directed learner model. He works not only with adademic institutions, but also with community resources to locate teachers. He's not afraid to try to teach himself when adequate resources cannot be found. Above all, Jeff has taken and will continue taking responsibility for his own education. I can't think of a better preparation for university life.

As independent confirmation of Jeff's attributes, we've attached a few letters of recommendation. We've also included supporting documents relating to awards, licenses, etc. Please call if you have questions.

Sincerely,

Cafi Cohen
Principal, Desert-Mountain Homeschool
[phone number]
Desert-Mountain Homeschool   10 January 1995
[address]

_____

Director of Admissions
Agnes Scott College
[address]

Re: Counselor Recommendation Form, Teacher Recommendation
Form, and Transcripts for Applicant Tamara Cohen [SSN]

Dear Sirs:

Tamara Cohen is high school senior in our home-based education
program. Although Tamara has a high school diploma from an independent-study school, American School, we will consider her graduated when she completes the requirements of Desert-Mountain
Homeschool, including college courses in which she is enrolled this
winter at Wright State University.

Approximately half of Tamara's high school work has been accom-
plished through American School. We've supplemented Tamara's
American School studies with our own courses, including Physical
Education, Spanish, Physics, and Introduction To Computers.
Tamara also took music courses and drama at Overland High School,
Aurora, CO. And, from February through October, 1994, she attend-
ed secondary school as an ASSE exchange student in Bendigo,
Victoria, Australia.

This information is summarized on the Desert-Mountain
Homeschool Transcript enclosed. With that are copies of the transcripts from American School and Overland High School. Official
transcripts are also being sent directly from these institutions.

Because the exchange program ended two weeks prior to the end of the school year in Australia, we have no transcript from that institution. We have included a semester evaluation from one of Tamara's Australian instructors.

Our homeschooling is best characterized by the word "eclectic". I am Tamara's parent and principal facilitator. "Teacher" would be an inappropriate designation because most of the time, Tamara teaches herself (with self-instructional materials) or find teachers in the community (for Bible Studies, our minister; for PE, a Tae Kwon Do instructor). Tamara and I jointly establish learning goals and try to locate the best resources in or out of the traditional school settings to accomplish these goals.

A sample day in our home-based program best serves to illustrate Tamara's motivation, intellectual qualities, academic achievement, maturity, and potential for growth. Last Tuesday, Tamara started her day by reading the newspaper. She then worked on physics for about 2 hours. We read the lesson together and discussed it; she did two problem sets and checked the answers. She then drove to her classes at Wright State University: Freshman Composition and Essentials of Public Address. That afternoon, following the classes, she worked three hours at a women's clothing store. Driving time amounted to an hour or more, time in which she listened to Spanish tapes.

On returning home, Tamara finished up the book she's been reading for a few days, *Animal Farm*. We discussed the plot and characters. Since 7th grade, Tamara's reading has been largely self-selected, ranging from recreational (Tom Clancy, John Grisham) to serious literature (*Much Ado About Nothing*, *The Grapes of Wrath*, *Proverbs*).

After helping with dinner, Tamara went to handbell practice and then joined some friends at church for volleyball. That evening at home, we discussed volunteer opportunities. Tamara's always had a volunteer job, and she's looking for a new one this spring. Right now what interests her most is working at a TV or radio station.

Tamara juggles a number of activities, and the line between the academic and non-academic becomes fuzzy at times. Our emphasis has been on self-directed learning, on learning how to learn, including learning to take advantage of a wide range of community resources. We think of our homeschool as a place where we are all learning all the time.

In her life organization skills and in her conduct with others, Tamara displays a high level of maturity. She successfully schedules and keeps up with a wide range of activities (see attached résumé). During her recent nine months in Australia, she adapted to a foreign host family, attended a foreign school, arranged her own travels and entertainment, and participated in school and community extracurriculars.

Tamara's strengths included her "people" skills, her organizational skills, her communication skills, and her creativity. She never finds herself in a room full of strangers. Regardless of the setting, she finds a way to fit in and to contribute. She also has the capacity to bring order out of chaos, especially in a group setting. In church youth groups, she is often elected to positions of authority because she seems to know intuitively how to delegate responsibility and accomplish goals.

Most importantly, Tamara is a self-directed learner. She works not just with academic institutions, but with community resources to locate teachers and mentors. She's had experience teaching herself when adequate resources cannot be found. Above all, Tamara has taken and will continue to take responsibility for her own education.

We've included a few letters of recommendation and supporting documentation for the résumé. Please call if you have questions.

Sincerely,

Cafi Cohen
Principal
Desert-Mountain Homeschool
[phone number]

APPENDIX C

RÈSUMÈS

We wrote these rèsumès together with our teenagers.

Jeffrey S. Cohen
[Social Security Number]
[Address]
[Phone Number]

[Date and place of birth]

Education

SAT Score: ___Verbal, ___ Math

Completed High School Credits

Math 5 1/2
English 5
Science 4
Social Sciences 5
Physical Education 1
Foreign Language 1
Miscellaneous 5

High School GPA: 4.0
High School Rank: 50/2000 at American School

Completed College Credits

Geology .4 semester credits

Computers .... .3 semester credits
Introduction to Engineering ... .4 quarter credits
Calculus I .... .4 quarter credits
University Physics .... .5 quarter credits

In-Progress High School Credits (1992-1993)

Math 1/2
Foreign Language 1
Pilot Training 1/2
Miscellaneous 2

In-Progress College Credits (University of Denver)

University Physics .... .5 quarter credits
Calculus .... .4 quarter credits

Activities

Civil Air Patrol (April, 1990 to present)
 —Ranks: Cadet Basic through Cadet Major
 —Cadet Commander of Mile Hi Cadet Squadron
 —Wrote articles for newsletter
 —Taught classes in Leadership, Aerospace, and Emergency
  Services
 —Earned Radio Operators' Permit
 —Completed Achievements: Curry, Arnold, Wright Brothers,
  Rickenbacker, Lindbergh, Doolittle, Goddard, Flight
  Commander, Public Affairs Officer, Logistics Officer,
  Operations Officer, and Leadership Officer
 —Instructor at Primary Training School on two occasions
 —Attended Colorado Wing Flight Training Encampment and
  completed first solo flight

—Attended Air Training Command Familiarization course at Mather AFB, California

Amateur Radio
—FCC Novice Class License (August, 1989)
—FCC Advanced Class License (November, 1991)
—Military Affiliate Radio System License (May, 1991)

Athletic Activities
—APR Rippers US Diving Team (October, 1991 to present)
—Self-devised conditioning program
—Distance running
—Upper body conditioning

Volunteer Work
—Military Affiliate Radio System, volunteer on traffic nets, pass MARS messages (May, 1991 to present)
—Hospital (September, 1990-May, 1991)

Miscellaneous
—Piano study, performance, and competitions
—Piano teaching

Awards

Civil Air Patrol
—Mitchell Award (July, 1991) for achieving a high level of aerospace knowledge in the CAP Cadet Program
—Earhart Award (July, 1992) for achieving a high level of knowledge of leadership in the CAP Cadet Program
—Solo Wings for soloing in a powered aircraft

Scholarships

—National Science Foundation Young Scholar (May, 1992) merit scholarship to attend "The Making Of An Engineer," at the University of Denver (June, 1992)
—Merit Scholarship awarded by the Mile Hi Cadet Squadron to attend the 1992 Colorado Wing Flight Training Encampment pilot training school

Miscellaneous
—National Piano Guild Auditions Superior Rating (May, 1992)
—New Mexico STEP content; first place awards in Scales, Ear Training, and Theory

Name: Tamara Gail Cohen   Address:
SSN: Phone:
Place of Birth: Date of Birth:

Education

SAT Score:

Completed High School Credits

Math	5
English	7
Science	3
Social Studies	5 1/2
Physical Education	3
Foreign Language	2
Miscellaneous	7

High School GPA: 3.95

High School Courses In Progress

Spanish II
Physics (AP)

College Courses In Progress

English 101
Communications 129

Activities

Foreign Exchange Student to Australia (1/94-10/94)
—Extensive independent travel

—Foreign paid work experience
—Attendance at overseas high school
—Cross-cultural interpersonal communication

Dramatic Arts and Choir
—Beginning Choir at Overland High School
—Advanced Women's Choir at Overland High School
—Director of beginning women's choir
—Part of musical *Grease* at Overland High School
—Part of musical *Oklahoma* at Bendigo Theater Co
—Instructor of beginning voice lessons
—Solo performances on piano
—Solo performances - singing
—Piano instruction
—Music theory instruction
—Section leader for Advanced Women's Choir

Church Activities
—President of Overland Bible Club
—Youth Group participation
—Youth Council participation
—Organizer of activities
—Participation in camps
—Choir (both youth and adult)
—Bell choir participation

Athletic Activities
—Tae Kwon Do
—Netball team in Australia
—Bush walking (Hiking) in Australia
—Miscellaneous sports: swimming, skiing, softball

WORK EXPERIENCE

Village Dry Cleaners
- —Taking in clothing
- —Tagging
- —Customer relations
- —Pressing shirts
- —Opening and closing duties
- —Using a cash register

Vocal Lessons
- —Maintaining student interest
- —Planning lesson materials
- —Modeling vocal techniques

Sizzler Restaurant
- —Greeting customers
- —Writing orders
- —Supplying drinks
- —Using the cash register
- —Waiting on tables
- —Maintaining salad bar
- —Maintaining general cleanliness
- —Assisting cooking staff
- —Closing and opening duties

Northern Reflections
- —Greeting customers
- —Selling clothing
- —Using the register
- —Maintaining store cleanliness
- —Opening and closing duties
- —Display design
- —Wardrobe coordination

VOLUNTEER EXPERIENCE

Humana Hospital
— Assisting nurses
—Transporting patients via wheelchair or bed
—Taking patient temperatures
—Various paperwork
—Responsibility for general cleanliness

Central Baptist Church
—Leading worship services
—Accompanying congregation on piano
—Computer data entry

Choral Directing
—Vocal warm-ups
— Piano accompanying
—Directing and giving advice where needed
—Picking appropriate music

Awards
—8th Gup Yellow Belt (Tae Kwon Do)
—7th Gup Yellow Belt with Green Stripe (Tae Kwon Do)
—4th Place at Ensemble Festival
—A Division Ladies Netball 2nd
—AA Division Mixed Netball 1st
—Humana Pin Volunteer Award

TWO APPLICATION ESSAYS

Our children wrote individual essays to each school they applied to. To read additional college application essays by homeschooled teenagers, see my website, www.homeschoolteenscollege.net.

WHY I WANT TO ATTEND A SERVICE ACADEMY
By Jeffrey S. Cohen

I pushed the throttle to the firewall. The engine of the Cessna 172 roared, and the airplane rolled down the runway. At 60 miles per hour, I pulled back on the control yoke, and the airplane lifted off the ground. Looking for approval from my instructor, I realized that the right seat was empty! This was the beginning of my first solo flight.

After that first takeoff, my confidence returned, and I flew the plane around the traffic pattern. However, during the descent to my first solo landing, I began to worry that I might have forgotten something. Were the flaps down? Was the carburetor heat on? Sure enough, I forgot to flare just before landing. All three wheels touched down at once, and airplane bounced off the runway. A little power stopped the porpoising motion. Then I closed the throttle, and skillfully landed the airplane—this time with a flare. I made two more successful takeoffs and landings that day.

I was apprehensive about soloing, but I was also eager to fly without an instructor. Ground school plus practice takeoffs and landings had given me assurance in the air. Soloing was exhilarating and gave me a great deal of confidence, not only in flying, but in other areas of my life. If I can fly an airplane, I can meet any challenge.

I received my flight training through the Civil Air Patrol (CAP), the US Air Force Auxiliary. CAP sponsors a cadet program to motivate American youth to participate in military and aerospace activities. Through participation in this military-oriented organization, I know that a career in the U.S. armed forces is for me. Soloing was the most exciting experience of my life. I want a military academy education because it will include the same types of experiences as my solo flight, and because it is the best preparation for a military career.

BLANKIE
By Tamara Cohen

Ahhhh....It smells just right. It's soft. It's warm. It waits for me at home. When I travel, it always gets packed. It comforts me no matter how many problems I have. It's perfect love. My blankie.

Before I was born, my grandmother, hoping for a girl, knitted a pink blanket about two feet square. Then she got to thinking about our family history. For several generations, only males have been born into the family. So, just to be safe Grandma added a baby blue lining around the blanket's edge. She figured a pink blanket with a blue border would be appropriate for either sex.

I still remember the days when my blankie was pretty and all in one piece, maybe up until I was 5 or 6 years old. Now it has gaping holes. The yarn has become brittle with age and use. It is shredded and stringy.

My blankie is definitely not the most flattering thing to keep around. I have had it since I was born; and, over the last ten years, I have only allowed it to be washed a few times. My boyfriend will not get near it. And my brother, well, let's just say my brother and my blankie do not have a close, personal relationship. My parents used to try to take it away from me, but through the years they've given up.

Blankies are highly under-rated in my opinion. Here are my top five reasons to keep one:

1. If you are a guest somewhere and your host has given you a flat pillow, a blankie is always a good substitute.
2. Blankies can go anywhere. Why not travel with a comforter that packs conveniently and that fits into any suitcase nook or cranny?

3. Blankies are great conversation starters. Mine usually makes people laugh, too. People quickly feel at ease with each other if they can share a laugh, especially over something like a blankie.

4. My blankie helps me judge character. Of those who catch a glimpse of the blanket, some will be polite and make no comment, some will joke about it, and some will say, "My goodness! Did your dog chew that thing up? It smells terrible!" Love me, love my blankie. I stay away from people who make disparaging comments. If a knitted scrap offends them, I do not want to deal with them.

5. My blankie reminds me of who I am and how much I have grown up. The older the blankie gets, the older I have gotten, the more educated I have become, and the more experiences I have had. My blankie reminds me of all the trials I have faced growing up. There is a shred for every challenge I have been nervous about facing and a knot for every situation I have tried to remedy.

So, for all those out there who are blankie-less, consider finding one for yourself or give one as a gift. Like I said, blankies are highly under-rated.

And What About College?

SAMPLE ECLECTIC CURRICULA

Here are outline descriptions of our teenagers' learning.

TAMARA'S EIGHTH GRADE PROGRAM

1. LIFE SCIENCE: Volunteer job at a veterinary clinic; tasks include taking vital signs on cats, dogs, horses; making up inoculations; collecting and preparing laboratory specimens; assisting biopsies and autopsies

2. MATH: *Saxon Algebra II*, one lesson and problem set alternating every other day with recreational math activities

3. ENGLISH/LANGUAGE ARTS: Daily student-selected reading; student daily journal; 4-H Public Speaking project; writing contests; correspondence

4. GEOGRAPHY: Geography board and computer games plus daily current events discussion

5. FINE ARTS: Piano lessons; voice lessons; church choir; 4-H Art project; volunteer with community drama group

6. PHYSICAL EDUCATION: Hiking, cycling, cross-country skiing, and Little League softball; Red Cross first-aid training

7. FOREIGN LANGUAGE: Russian self-instructional course; 2 Russian pen pals; unit study on Russian history

8. HOME ECONOMICS: Daily household tasks including meal planning and preparation and gardening; paid child-care; two 4-H sewing projects

9. RELIGIOUS STUDIES: Weekly Sunday school plus Christian principles and comparative religion study with youth group

JEFFREY'S ELEVENTH GRADE PROGRAM

1. MATH: *Saxon Advanced Mathematics* one lesson daily plus math games

2. SCIENCE: Electronics with local amateur radio club; Rocketry projects with Civil Air Patrol; Geology class with local community college; American School Chemistry class

3. ENGLISH: Self-selected reading plus daily journal; articles for the Civil Air Patrol newsletter; speeches for Civil Air Patrol; American School English Literature course

4. SOCIAL STUDIES: Economics (*What Ever Happened To Penny Candy?*); current events reading and discussion; unit study on US Constitution; video history documentaries; World War II unit study

5. FINE ARTS: Piano lessons and piano teaching; church choir

6. PHYSICAL EDUCATION: Diving team; hiking and cycling; self-devised personal conditioning program

7. FOREIGN LANGUAGE: American School Spanish course

8. COMPUTER SCIENCE: Introductory computer course at junior college

9. INDEPENDENT LIVING SKILLS: Daily household chores and yard work

And What About College?

SELECTIVE COLLEGES THAT HAVE ADMITTED HOME-SCHOOLERS

This is a partial list. It includes schools I have learned about through published reports or personal communications, either from admitted students or from the colleges themselves. For a much longer list, check Karl Bunday's excellent website, www.learninfreedom.colleges_4_hmsc.html, and look for "Colleges That Admit Homeschoolers FAQ."

Competitiveness ratings (based on *Barron's Profiles of American Colleges*) are: ***Most Competitive, **Highly Competitive, *Very Competitive.

*	Agnes Scott College, Georgia
**	Amherst College, Massachusetts
*	Austin College, Texas
**	Boston University, Massachusetts
**	Brigham Young University, Utah
**	Brown University, Rhode Island
***	California Institute of Technology, California
*	Calvin College, Michigan
**	Carleton College, Minnesota
**	Carnegie-Mellon University, Pennsylvania
*	Christendom College, Virginia
***	Cornell University, New York
*	Covenant College, Georgia
***	Dartmouth College, New Hampshire
**	GMI Engineering and Management Institute, Michigan
*	Grand Valley State University, Michigan

**	Grove City College, Pennsylvania
*	Harding University, Arkansas
***	Harvard University, Massachusetts
***	Haverford College, Pennsylvania
*	Hillsdale College, Michigan
*	Houghton College, New York
*	John Brown University, Arkansas
**	Kenyon College, Ohio
*	Loyola College, Maryland
***	Massachusetts Institute of Technology, Massachusetts
*	Messiah College, Pennsylvania
***	Middlebury College, Vermont
*	Mississippi State University, Mississippi
*	Oakland University, Michigan
**	Oberlin College, Ohio
*	Oklahoma State University, Oklahoma
***	Oxford University, United Kingdom
**	Pennsylvania State University, Pennsylvania
*	Pepperdine University, California
***	Princeton University, New Jersey
**	Rensselaer Polytechnic Institute, New York
***	Rice University, Texas
**	Rose-Hulman Institute of Technology, Indiana
*	State University of New York, Buffalo, New York
***	Swarthmore College, Pennsylvania
*	Taylor University, Indiana
**	Thomas Aquinas College, California
***	United States Air Force Academy, Colorado
***	United States Naval Academy, Maryland
*	University of Alabama, Huntsville, Alabama
*	University of Colorado, Boulder, Colorado
**	University of California, Berkeley, California
**	University of California, Los Angeles, California
*	University of California, Santa Cruz, California
***	University of Chicago, Illinois

*	University of Dallas, Texas
*	University of Evansville, Indiana
**	University of Michigan, Michigan
**	University of Minnesota, Minnesota
*	University of Missouri, Kansas City, Missouri
*	University of Missouri, Rolla, Missouri
**	University of North Carolina, North Carolina
*	University of Texas, Austin, Texas
***	University of Virginia, Virginia
*	University of Washington, Washington
**	University of Wisconsin, Wisconsin
**	Vanderbilt University, Tennessee
*	Virginia Wesleyan College, Virginia
**	Washington University Medical Center, Missouri
**	Wheaton College, Illinois
**	Whitworth College, Washington
***	Williams College, Massachusetts
**	Worcester Polytechnic Institute, Massachusetts
***	Yale University, Connecticut

And What About College?

COLLEGES OF SPECIAL INTEREST TO HOMESCHOOLERS

Listed below are commonly overlooked schools that—for a variety of reasons—warrant the attention of home educators.

Antioch College
Yellow Springs, OH 45387
937-767-7331; 800-543-9436
college.antioch.edu
Co-op program — all students spend half their time on campus, half their time working/interning in the real world.

Bard College
Annandale-on-Hudson, NY 12504
914-758-7472
www.bard.edu
Highly individualized programs. Student's compatibility with educational philosophy of the school more important than numbers (SAT, GPA); SAT is optional.

Berea College
Berea, KY 40404
606-985-3000; 800-326-5948
www.berea.edu
Such a deal, if you can get in. Except for a small fee, all expenses paid with scholarships for all admitted students. All students work on campus part-time.

College of the Ozarks
Point Lookout, MO 65726
417-334-6411; 800-222-0525
www.cofo.edu
Another great deal. All student tuition paid for with on-campus, part-time jobs, and scholarships.

Colorado College
Colorado Springs, CO 80903
719-389-6344; 800-542-7214
www.cc.colorado.edu
Block plan scheduling only. Students take one class at a time for 3-1/2 weeks, move on to the next class. Mostly seminars, few lectures.

Cooper Union For The Advancement of Science and Art
New York, NY 10003-7183
212-353-4120
www.cooper.edu
Engineering, art, and architecture majors only. Tuition is free; students pay fees and room and board.

Deep Springs College
Deep Springs, CA
HC 72 Box 45001
Dyer, NV 89010
760-872-2000
deepsprings.edu
Small, selective men's two-year college. All expenses paid. Classes and seminars in the morning, ranch work in the afternoon. Graduates transfer to Harvard, Yale, etc.

DigiPen Institute of Technology
Redmond, WA 98052 & Vancouver, BC
425-558-0299

www.digipen.edu
New college offering AS and BS degrees for video game programmers and 3-D computer animators. Also offer high school summer workshops.

Drury College
Springfield, MO 65802
417-865-8731; 800-922-2274
www.drury.edu
Church-affiliated school that schedules a 3-year baccalaureate degree for some majors; traditional academics; very reasonably priced.

Evergreen State College
Olympia, WA 98505
360-866-6000
www.evergreen.edu
Public school with PhD's teaching in seminar settings; original works, no textbooks; evaluation with portfolio assessments, no grades.

Goddard College
Plainfield, VT 05667
802-454-8311; 800-468-4888
www.goddard.edu
Classes consist of small discussion groups; no grades or exams. Appeals to creative, independent students. No standardized test (SAT or ACT) required.

Grove City College
Grove City, PA 16127-2104
724-458-2100
www.gcc.edu
Conservative, spiritual, intensely academic school. Traditional academics; very reasonably priced.

Hampshire College
Amherst, MA 01002
413-559-5471
www.hampshire.edu
No tests, grades, credits, or majors; instead course papers, self/teacher evaluations, concentrations; SAT not required.

Kettering University (formerly GMI Engineering and Management Institute)
Flint, Michigan 48504
800-955-4464
www.gmi.edu
Students alternate academic and work experience semesters at this conservative business-engineering school.

New College of the University of South Florida
Sarasota, Florida 34243-2197
941-359-4269
www.newcollege.usf.edu
Intense academic atmosphere at a bargain price. A Money Magazine best college buy. Students design their own courses of study. Written evaluations, no grades.

Oglethorpe University
Atlanta, Georgia 30319
800-428-4484, ext 8443
www.oglethorpe.edu
Small liberal arts college in big city. Good balance of small class sizes and top quality professors.

Patrick Henry College
Purcellville, Virginia 20134
540-338-1776
www.phu.edu
Accepting its first students in summer of the year 2000. Provides a

Bible-centered academically rigorous education together with extensive apprenticeships.

Rose-Hulman Institute of Technology
Terre Haute, Indiana 47803
812-877-1511; 800-878-7448
www.rose-hulman.edu
Engineering and science school with integrated curriculum first two years combining all subjects into a single course. Many of the professors homeschool their own children.

St. John's College
Annapolis, MD 21404
410-263-2371; 800-727-9238
Santa Fe, NM 87501
505-984-6000; 800-331-5232
www.sjca.edu
One college, two campuses. Classical, structured curriculum based on the Great Books of western civilization; discussion-oriented classes.

Simon's Rock College
Great Barrington, MA 01230-9702
413-528-7317; 800-235-7186
www.simons-rock.edu
Four-year college wholly devoted to early admission. Most students enroll after completing 10th or 11th grade. Independent studies and creative arts majors are popular.

United States Merchant Marine Academy
Kings Point, NY 11024
516-773-5000; 800-732-6267
www.usmma.edu
No tuition or room and board payments. Academy expenses covered by earnings at sea. Majors include engineering, marine engineering, transportation management.

See also Appendix H for contact information for the four military service academies.

A FEW POINTERS ON APPLYING TO A SERVICE ACADEMY

By Col. Terrell Cohen, Ret. USAF, Air Force Academy Admission Liaison Officer since 1997.

1. The military academies pay for all educational and living expenses. Nevertheless, students should apply only if they want careers as military officers. Do not encourage your student to apply just for the free education. Programs are academically and physically rigorous. Military discipline is constant. Those not fully committed are weeded out. Graduates incur a pay back obligation of at least four years of active duty military service.

2. The student, not the parents, should make all contacts with the academies—letters, telephone calls, and so on. Academy admissions personnel want to speak directly with applicants, not parents. During the application process, the academies assign liaison officers and regional admissions personnel to each applicant. Make sure the student keeps a telephone log of all conversations.

3. Check out summer sports and academic programs the academies offer for high school juniors and seniors. Through these programs, students preview the military academy environment. Also, academy officials get to know students. Also, during the school year, prospective students may schedule day or overnight visits, which provide opportunities to attend classes and talk with cadets and midshipmen.

4. Get answers to important questions directly from the academy admissions officers. Because policies change, sometimes recruiters, high school counselors, current students, other successful applicants, congressional office personnel, and liaison officers (military officers and others who do student interviews) do not know the whole story.

5. Prepare academically. Write to the service academies to get a list of required high school subjects. Competition is fierce. Exceed this list! One-third to one-half of those admitted have college credit. Homeschooled students should consider taking several college classes during the high school junior and senior years.

6. Prepare physically. Roughly 85% of those admitted to the academies have lettered in a high school sport. The academy programs are physically rigorous. The fitness testing screens out those in poor physical condition.

Students should train in an individual sport or participate in a team sport. Homeschoolers without access to high school sports programs should investigate those at YMCA's, Parks and Recreation Departments, Civil Air Patrol, and so on. Private and group lessons are also an option for certain sports—gymnastics and martial arts, for example. In the absence of any of these opportunities, remember that anyone can individually train for and run road races as a sport.

Our son Jeff participated on a U.S. Diving team at the local Parks and Recreation Department. Much to our surprise, the West Point diving coach telephoned him several times and indicated he was interested in recruiting Jeff for college diving.

7. Admissions includes a physical fitness test. Obtain information on this test from the academy admissions offices, and plan to train for the physical fitness test for several months. All academy applicants should implement a personal physical conditioning program (aerobic and weight training) throughout the high school years.

8. Prepare for leadership with Civil Air Patrol, Scouting, 4-H, and other community groups. Students need several years of experience these groups to rise to leadership roles. The Civil Air Patrol Cadet Program (check telephone book white pages or a nearby Air Force installation) is particularly appropriate. Students receive training in aerospace and aviation and in military customs and courtesies. They rise through ranks similar to those used by the Air Force.

9. Apply early, beginning the process in the spring of what would be the student's junior year. Write or call and ask for materials then. The process involves interviews, mailings, physical tests, medical tests, and more. Do everything as early as possible. Things do go awry, and you will need time to fix them.

10. During the application process, be persistent and followup on problems immediately. At one point our son Jeff received a letter stating he was medically disqualified from admission to any academy. "We regret to inform you that you are no longer a candidate for an appointment.... Good luck in your future endeavors."

DODMERB (Department of Defense Medical Examination Review Board) does the medical screening for all the academies. They had based their decision on a single aberrant laboratory test. By investigating, we learned that the reporting laboratory had made a clerical error. It was our job to check this out; DODMERB would never have done it. Think of the admissions process like dodging bullets on a firing range. Applicants who dodge all the bullets win appointments.

11. You will also need a nomination from the President, Vice President, or a member of Congress. The academies then consider nominees for actual appointments (acceptance). Specific instructions to apply for nominations come with the academy application materials. Homeschoolers follow these instructions, the same as everyone else.

12. Take standardized tests early, the PSAT at the beginning of the

junior year and the SAT at the end of the junior year. While not required, Advanced Placement and SAT II (Achievement Test) scores enhance the student's academic profile.

13. Apply to all of the academies. The student may only be interested in one branch of the military. Every year, though, a few graduates of each of the academies end up serving their payback time in a different branch of the service. For example, a Naval Academy midshipman could end up serving in the Air Force. Although each academy is unique, all offer a top-notch education.

14. Also apply for Reserve Officer Training Corps (ROTC) scholarships offered by the Air Force, Army, Navy, and Marines. ROTC scholarships pay a substantial proportion of expenses at civilian colleges and universities. Some ROTC scholarship offers are comparable with the academy offers — in other words, all expenses paid. Military recruiters and colleges that have ROTC programs will supply you with appropriate forms.

15. Do not give up. Many students win admission to the academies after a year or two of college elsewhere. Re-apply, if that is what the student really wants. The academies also have several slots each year for military enlisted personnel.

16. An excellent reference book for applying to the US Air Force Academy is *The Air Force Academy Candidate Book* by William Smallwood.

Academy Contacts:

United States Air Force Academy
USAFA, CO 80840-5025
719-333-1110
www.usafa.af.mil

HOMESCHOOLERS' COLLEGE PLANNING CHECKLIST

Grade 9

___Plan a full homeschooling schedule around the student's interests, talents, and goals; document everything.

___Include foreign language study if the student does not already have competency equivalent to two years of high school study.

___Include SAT and ACT preparation materials in the curriculum.

___During vacations, visit several college campuses.

___Research colleges that offer special programs (work-study, co-op arrangements with businesses, learning disabilities accommodations, and so on).

___Request letters of recommendation from anyone who has worked with the student (employers, coaches, music instructors, church leaders, youth group leaders, etc.).

___Have the student keep a daily or weekly journal of activities and events; this material may eventually be used as the basis of an application essay.

—Contact several colleges and ask about their policies for evaluating and admitting homeschoolers.

___At the end of the year, write a transcript, course descriptions, and résumé.

Grade 10

___Reassess goals and priorities and re-evaluate curriculum and activities.

___Continue or begin foreign language study.

___Include SAT or ACT preparation materials in the curriculum.

___Take the PSAT in October (make arrangements for this at a local school in late August or early September); students may take the PSAT as sophomores and juniors; the score obtained the next to last year of high school counts for National Merit Scholarship consideration.

___If the student will be applying to selective schools, s/he should study for and plan to take an SAT II Subject Test (Achievement Test) in the spring. Save the Writing and Math Achievement Tests for later; prepare for and take one this year in Biology, American History and Social Studies, or a foreign language.

___Consider taking one college class through the local junior college or through a correspondence program.

___Contact several college admissions offices for viewbooks (general information brochures); visit those that look interesting.

___Request letters of recommendation.

___Student should keep a daily or weekly journal of activities and events.

___At the end of the year, write or update the transcript, course descriptions, and résumé.

Grade 11

___Assess accomplishments and the impression the transcript and résumé make; compare with college requirements and make adjustments; for consideration at selective colleges, exceed the recommended list.

___Include foreign language study in the program.

___Continue to practice for the SAT or ACT.

___Take the PSAT in the fall.

___Take the SAT in the spring of the junior year.

___For applications to selective schools, begin practice for Writing and Math SAT II Subject Tests.

___If the student will be applying to selective schools, s/he should plan to take an SAT II Subject test if he did not take one the previous year.

___Take one or more college classes.

___Query colleges, especially local ones and those in which the student is interested, about special school-year and summer academic and sports programs for high school junior and seniors; have the student attend one, if possible.

___Attend college fairs.

___Make a list of six to ten colleges that most interest the student; with research, whittle this list down to three to six to which s/he will apply; call for application materials; make sure the student is on their mailing lists.

___Student should continue making journal entries; in the spring, review these entries for possible college application essay topics.

___Request letters of recommendation.

___Write or update the transcript, course descriptions, and resume.

Grade 12

___Review college entrance requirements again; make adjustments as needed to your program.

___If you have not previously done so, obtain application materials and financial aid materials from all colleges to which the student plans to apply.

___If applicable, obtain ROTC application materials.

___Make a calendar on which the student records interview and school tour dates, college fair dates, and deadlines for standardized test registrations, application submissions, merit scholarships, financial aid statements, and so on.

___Allow at least one month to write each application essay;

begin essays as soon as the student has the applications; plan on many rewrites and have several people review them.

____If the student has not taken the SAT or ACT, register to take the test as soon as possible; if the student is not satisfied with a previous score, schedule a re-test.

____Plan to take one or more college courses.

____Complete federal and state tax returns as early as possible; information is needed for financial aid forms.

____Contact colleges and arrange for day or overnight visits so the student can attend classes and talk with students already enrolled.

____If the student will be applying to a very competitive school, plan to take the SAT II Writing and Math achievement tests in the fall.

____Prior to submitting applications, update the transcript and course descriptions; include in-progress courses and planned courses for the spring.

____Prior to submitting applications, update the résumé.

____Request additional letters of recommendation, if needed or if they have not been requested previously.

____Research additional college scholarships offered by local groups; note deadlines on the calendar.

And What About College?

RESOURCES

Below find resources that we and other homeschooling families have found the most helpful. Inclusion does not imply endorsement.

To locate most books, try your library (Inter-Library Loan), special order from a local bookstore, or www.amazon.com. Most large bookstores stock many of the titles.

Internet addresses (which you should prefix with "http://") are the most recent available, but may have changed by the time you read this. If so, use web search engines like Google (www.google.com), and enter the name of the institution, book, or author as a primary search term. If you don't have a computer, check applicable web sites on the Internet at the library.

SOME DIPLOMA-GRANTING PROGRAMS

Check the Homeschool-Teens-College website for updates: www.homeschoolteenscollege.net

Abbington Hills School, Suite 6-152, 2140 Route 88, Bricktown, NJ 08724, 732-892-4475; www.abbingtonhillschool.com

A Beka Home School, Station HE, Pensacola, FL 32523-6030, 800-874-BEKA; www.abeka.com

Academy of Home Education, Bob Jones University, Greenville, SC 29614, 864-242-5100, ext 2047; www.bju.edu/press/home.html

Alger Learning Center Independence High School, 121 Alder Dr., Sedro Woolley, WA 98284; 800-595 2630. www.independent-learning.com

American School, 2200 E. 170th St., Lansing, IL 60438, 708-418-2800 or 800 531-9268; www.iit.edu/~american

Branford Grove School, PO Box 341172, Arleta, CA 91334, 818-890-0350; www.branfordgrove.com

Brigham Young University Independent-Study High School, 206 Harman Building, PO Box 21514, Provo, UT 84602, 801-378-2868. www.coned.byu.edu/is/hsch.htm

Cambridge Academy, 33000 SW 34th Ave., Suite 102, Ocala, FL 34474 800-252-3777. www.home-school.com/Mall/CambridgeAcad.html

Christa McAuliffe Academy, 3601 W. Washington Ave., Yakima, WA 98903, 509-575-4989; www.cmacademy.org

Christian Liberty Academy, 502 W. Euclid Ave., Arlington Heights, IL 60004, 800-348-0899; www.class.kingshighway.com

Chrysalis School, Inc., 14241 NE Woodinville-Duvall Rd., #243, Woodinville, WA 98072; www.wolfe.net/~chrysali

Citizens High School, 188 College Drive, Orange Park, FL 32067, 904-276-1700; www.citizenschool.com

Clonlara Home-Based Education Program and Clonlara CompuHigh, 1289 Jewett St., Ann Arbor, MI 48104, 734-769-4515. www.clonlara.org

Dennison On-Line Internet School, Box 29781, Los Angeles, CA 90029-0781, 323-662-3226; www.dennisononline.com

Eagle Christian School, 2526 Sunset Lane, Missoula, MT 59804, 888-324-5348; www.valleychristian.org

HCL Boston School, PO Box 2920, Big Bear City, CA 92314, 909-585-7188; www.bostonschool.org

Hewitt Homeschooling Resources, Box 9, Washougal, WA 98671, 800-348-1750; www.homeeducation.org

Home Study International, 12501 Old Columbia Pike, Silver Spring, MD 20904. 800-782-4769; www.his.edu

ICS/Newport/Pacific High School, 925 Oak St., Scranton, PA 18515, 800-238-9525 ext 7496; www.icslearn.com

Institute for the Study of the Liberal Arts and Sciences (Scholar's Online Academy and Regina Coeli Academy), 9755 E. McAndrew Ct., Tucson, AZ 85748, 520-751-1942; www.islas.org

Internet Academy, 32020 1st Avenue South, Federal Way, WA 98003, 253-945-2004; www.iacademy.org

Keystone National High School, 420 W. Fifth St., Bloomsburg, PA 17815, 800-255-4937; www.keystonehighschool.com

Kolbe Academy, 1600 F Street, Napa, CA 94559, 707-255-6499. www.community.net/~kolbe

Laurel Springs High School, 1002 E. Ojai Ave., Ojai, CA 93024, 800-377-5890. www.laurelsprings.com

North Atlantic Regional High School, 116 Third Avenue, Auburn, ME 04210, 800-882-2828, Ext. 16. www.homeschoolassociates.com/NARS

North Dakota Division of Independent Study, 701-231-6000. www.dis.dpi.state.nd.us/

NorthStar Academy, 22571 Wye Road, Sherwood Park, Alberta, Canada T8C 1H9, 888-464-6280; www.northstar-academy.org

Oak Meadow School, PO Box 740 Putney, VT 05346, 802-387-2021. www.oakmeadow.com

Phoenix Academies, 1717 West Northern Avenue, Suite 104, Phoenix, AZ 85017-5469; www.phoenixacademies.org

Richard M. Milburn High School, 14416 Jefferson Davis Highway, Suite 12, Woodbridge, VA 22191, 703-494-0147

Royal Academy, PO Box 1056, Gray, Maine 04039, 207-657-2800. www.homeeducator.com/HEFS/royalacademy.htm

School of Tomorrow, PO Box 1438, Lewisville, TX 75067, 800-925-7777; www.schooloftomorrow.com

Seton Home Study School, 1350 Progress Dr., Front Royal, VA 22630, 540-636-9990; www.setonhome.org

St. Thomas Aquinas Academy, PO Box 630, Ripon, CA 95366, 209-599-0665; www.staa-homeschool.com

Summit Christian Academy, 2100 N. Hwy 360, Suite 503, Grand Prairie, TX 75050, 800-362-9180; scahomeschool.com

Sycamore Tree, 2179 Meyer Place, Costa Mesa, CA 92627, 949-650-4466; www.sycamoretree.com

Texas Tech University Division of Continuing Education, Box 42191, Lubbock, TX 79409, 806-742-2352, ext 232; www.dce.ttu.edu

University of Nebraska, Lincoln Independent Study High School,

33rd & Holdrege Sts., Lincoln, NE 68583, 402-472-4321. www.unl.edu/conted/disted/ishs.html

Westbridge Academy, 1610 W. Highland Ave., Box 228, Chicago, IL 60660, 773-743-3312; www.flash.net/~wx30/chp

GENERAL HOMESCHOOLING

Holt Associates/*Growing Without Schooling* magazine, 2380 Massachusetts Ave., Suite 104, Cambridge, MA 02140, 617 864-3100. Free catalog and order line: call 888-925-9298; www.holtgws.com

Home Education Magazine, PO Box 1083, Tonasket WA 98855. Free info packet: 800-236-3278; www.home-ed-magazine.com

The Homeschooling Book of Answers edited by Linda Dobson (1998, Prima Publishing); answers to eighty-eight commonly asked questions by some of homeschooling's most respected voices.

Homeschool Resource Guide. This is a website with detailed listings for curriculum, supplementary materials, and supplies: members.home.net/ct-homeschool/guide.htm

Homeschool Support On The Internet. Great index of chat groups, email loops, resources, and support groups: www.geocities.com/Athens/8259

Homeschooling Today, PO Box 1608, Fort Collins, CO 80522-1608, 954-962-1930; www.homeschooltoday.com

Homeschool World/*Practical Homeschooling*, Homeschool World is the company and website, home of *Practical Homeschooling*, the magazine. Lots of great articles on-line at: www.home-school.com

Jon's Homeschool Page. One of the older indexes of homeschooling information on the Internet, lots of unschooling articles: www.midnightbeach.com/hs

Kaleidoscapes Homeschool Discussion Board. Discussion boards for general home education, special needs, unit studies, curriculum and much more: www.kaleidoscapes.com/wwwboard

National Home Education Research Institute, PO Box 13939, Salem, OR 97309, 503-364-1490; www.nheri.org

Yahoo Homeschool Page:
www.yahoo.com/Education/K_12/Alternative/Home_Schooling

HIGH SCHOOL UNIT STUDY PROGRAMS

Far Above Rubies, Family Christian Academy, 487 Myatt Dr., Madison, TN 38115, 800-788-0840; www.heartofwisdom.com

KONOS, PO Box 250, Anna, TX 75409, 972-924-2712; www.konos.com

SCOPE & SEQUENCE REFERENCES

A Beka Books Scope and Sequence Nursery through Grade Twelve, 800-874-BEKA:
www.abeka.com/ABB/Resources/98-9ScpSeq.pdf

Practical Homeschooling, summer 1995 issue has 5 different high school scope and sequences, www.home-school.com

Science Scope and Guides To History by Kathryn Stout, Design-A-Study, 408 Victoria Ave., Wilmington, DE 19804, www.designastudy.com

Standard US Homeschool Curriculum:
www.euschool.com/curric1.html

Trivium Suggested Course of Study:
www.muscanet.com/~trivium/ttt/tttsuggested.html

Utah State Core Curriculum:
www.uen.org/cgi-bin/websql/utahlink/CoreHome.hts

World Book Encyclopedia *Typical Course of Study Kindergarten through Grade 12* by William H. Nault, 800-621-8202:
www.worldbook.com/EduGuide/vjs/curr.html

HOMESCHOOLING TEENAGERS

The Big Book of Home Learning 4th Edition, Volume 3, Junior High through High School by Mary Pride (1999, Home Life, Inc.). Excellent reviews of formal and non-traditional learning resources.

The Christian Home Educators' Curriculum Manual: Junior and Senior High, 2nd Ed. by Cathy Duffy (1997-98, Grove). Resource reviews and recommendations for grades 7-12.

College Admissions: A Guide For Homeschoolers by Judy Gelner (1990). Relates how homeschooled son Kendall's admission to Rice University with no transcript and no diploma.

Homeschooling For Excellence by David & Micki Colfax (1988, Warner Books). Down-to-earth eclectic homeschooling that sent three sons to Harvard.

Homeschooling The High Schooler, Volumes 1 and 2, by Diana McAlister and Candice Oneschak (1993, Family Academy Publications, 146 SW 153rd #289, Seattle, WA 98166).

Homeschooling: The Teen Years, by Cafi Cohen (2000, Prima Publishing). Specifics on choosing and planning curriculum and addressing a host of other challenges relevant to educating teenagers at home.

Homeschool-Teens-College. More information on homeschooling ages 11–18 plus college admissions for homeschoolers, includes college application essays written by homeschooled teenagers: www.homeschoolteenscollege.net

Kaleidoscapes High School and College Web-based discussion board, all are welcome: www.kaleidoscapes.com/colleges

No Regrets: How Homeschooling Earned Me A Master's Degree At Age 16 by Alexandra Swann (1989, Cygnet Press). The title says it all; traditional approach.

Real Lives: 11 Teenagers Who Don't Go To School edited by Grace Llewellyn (1993, Lowry House). Essays by 11 homeschooled teenagers.

Senior High: A Home-Designed Form+U+la by Barbara Edtl Shelton (1996, Homeschool Seminars and Publications, 182 No. Columbia Heights Rd., Longview, WA 98632); personalized record keeping, creative approaches.

A Sense of Self: Listening To Homeschooled Adolescent Girls by Susannah Sheffer (1995, Heinemann). Read a hopeful picture of adolescence.

The Teenage Liberation Handbook by Grace Llewellyn (1998, Lowry House); self-directed learning, college without high school, volunteering, apprenticeships.

COLLEGE NOW?

The Off-The-Beaten-Path Job Book: You CAN Make a Living AND Have A Life! by Sandra Gurvis (1995, Citadel Press). Details no-college-required jobs like Greeting Card Writer, Polygrapher, Midwife, Product Tester, and more.

The Question Is College: On Finding and Doing Work You Love by Herbert Kohl (1998, Heinemann). Explore career and college options with this open-ended inquiry; good appendix for exploring non-college careers.

Real People, Real Jobs: Reflecting Your Interests In The World of Work by David H. Montross et. al. (1995, Consulting Psychologists Press). Stories of real people in traditional and not-so-traditional occupations.

What Color Is Your Parachute? by Richard Bolles (Ten Speed Press, updated annually). Job/career hunting manual for those who don't expect to go to college and those who need to determine if college is necessary.

COLLEGE ADMISSIONS TESTING

ACT: ACT Registration, PO Box 414, Iowa City, IA 52243, 319-337-1270; www.act.org

FairTest: National Center for Fair and Open Testing, 342 Broadway, Cambridge, MA 02139, 617 864-4810, www.fairtest.org; list of SAT-optional colleges and universities nationwide.

PSAT: Given only in October through private and public high schools; contact a high school counselor's office in August or early

September for registration information; for general information, call 609-771-7300

SAT I and SAT II: College Board SAT, Princeton, NJ 08541, 609-771-7600; www.collegeboard.org

COLLEGE CREDIT BY EXAMINATION

College Level Examination Program (CLEP): *The Official Handbook For The CLEP Examinations* published by The College Board, PO Box 6601, Princeton, NJ 08541. www.collegeboard.org

The Advanced Placement Program (AP), The College Board, 45 Columbus Avenue, New York, NY 10023. www.collegeboard.org

PREPARATION FOR COLLEGE ENTRANCE TESTS

Barron's How To Prepare for the ACT: American College Testing Assessment Program, 10th Edition, by George Ehrencraft et.al. (1998, Barron's)

The College Board has a searchable college database plus in-depth information on the SAT, PSAT, CLEP, and AP tests; preparation tips; SAT question of the day; sample tests, and more: www.collegeboard.org

Cracking The SAT and PSAT 2000 (Annual) by Adam Robinson and Jon Katzman (1999, The Princeton Review); www.review.com

Cracking The SAT and PSAT With Sample Tests on CD-ROM by Adam Robinson and Jon Katzman (1999, The Princeton Review); www.review.com

Cracking The SAT II: English Subject Tests 1999-2000 (and similar titles for other subjects) by Elizabeth Buffer, et. al. (1999, The Princeton Review); www.review.com

10 Real SATS edited by Cathy Claman (1997, College Entrance Examination Board)

RESEARCHING COLLEGES

Barron's Profiles of American Colleges (2000, Barron's Educational Series)

The Best 311 Colleges: 2000 Edition, edited by Edward T. Custard (1999, Princeton Review); www.review.com

College and University Homepages. Alphabetical and geographic links to institutions worldwide plus FAQ's:
www.mit.edu:8001/people/cdemello/univ.html

Colleges for Homeschoolers, Karl Bunday's updated list of colleges that have accepted homeschoolers:
www.learninfreedom.org/colleges_4_hmsc.html

The Fiske Guide To Colleges 2000, by Edward Fiske (1999, Times Books)

Princeton Review College Search & Test Information. College search by major, size, etc. plus information on the SAT, PSAT, and other tests; discussion groups: www.review.com

Your Best College Buys Now issued annually, in the fall, by Money Magazine; check for it on newsstands

HOMESCHOOLING COLLEGE

Bear's Guide To Earning College Degrees Nontraditionally, 13th Edition, by John Bear and Mariah Bear (1999, Ten Speed Press).

College Degrees By Mail and Internet by John Bear (1999, Ten Speed Press)

College On-Line: How To Take College Courses Without Leaving Home by James P. Duffy (1997, John Wiley and Sons)

The Independent Study Catalog, 7th Edition, (1998, Peterson's Guides); www.petersons.com

The Internet University: College Courses by Computer by Dan Corrigan (1996, Cape Software Press); www.caso.com

Peterson's Guide To Distance Learning Programs, 2000 (1999, Peterson's Guides); www.petersons.com

Virtual College: A Quick Guide to How You Can Get the Degree You Want With Computer, TV, Video, Audio, and other Distance Learning Tools edited by Pam Dixon (1996, Peterson's Guides); www.petersons.com

FINANCIAL AID

College Costs and Financial Aid Handbook 2000 (Serial) by College Scholarship Service (1999, College Entrance Examination Board)

College Financial Aid for Dummies, by Helm Davis and Joyce Lain Kennedy (1999, IDG Books)

Debt-Free College, by Gordon Wadsworth (1999, Financial Aid Information Services)

Financial Aid Information Page; FAQ's, telephone numbers, links to college financial aid offices, newsgroups, and mailing lists: www.cs.cmu.edu/afs.cs/user/mkant/Public/FinAid/finaid.html

US Department of Education Student Guide; exhaustive financial aid information; eligibility, application procedures, deadlines, and telephone numbers: www.ed.gov/prog_info/SFA/StudentGuide

MISCELLANEOUS

Initial Eligibility Procedures for Homeschooled Student Athletes; NCAA certification process for homeschooled athletes: www.ncaa.org/cbsa/home_school.html

On-line Advanced Placement Courses, available to homeschoolers nationwide from the Pennsylvania Homeschoolers' Association. Pennsylvania Homeschoolers, RR2, Box 117, Kittanning, PA, 16201; www.pahomeschoolers.com/courses

Not Back To School Camp, camp in Oregon run by Grace Llewellyn (*Teenage Liberation Handbook* author) each August; camp attracts homeschoolers nationwide. Genius Tribe, PO Box 1014, Eugene, OR 97440; www.geocities.com/Athens/7325

After-the-Fact Curriculum or How to Take the Drudgery Out of High School Record Keeping

By Terri Endsley

When our teenaged son and daughter began home educating three and a half years ago, we had many questions about record-keeping and what counted for academic credit. Since we were enrolled with Clonlara School, in Ann Arbor, MI, we initially followed their form and suggestions, finally evolving into the record-keeping format we used for our daughter. The fact that there is no one right way to keep records is both reassuring and unnerving. However, the following is an explanation of our final, and to us, most satisfying record-keeping format.

For the first month, high school-aged homeschoolers should keep an extremely detailed journal of everything they do (except personal grooming). List every daily activity from household chores, shopping, errands, jobs, phone calls, books, magazines, and newspapers, TV shows, movies, time spent with family, friends, pets, preparing snacks and meals, walking, bike riding, sports, letter writing, journal writing, trips, field trip activities—EVERYTHING—and the approximate amount of time spent on each activity. This journal is not meant to be a personal diary. Keeping one of those is fun too, but that is not what this journal is for. Do not necessarily try to do school activities; do what interests you. After this first month of detailed record-keeping the student will not need to keep such detailed records, because the time spent on many activities can be averaged.

At the end of the first month, go through this journal and assign a broad subject category to every activity. We did not assign credit for "junk" TV, phone conversations with friends, and parties. But we did, for awhile, keep track of those hours under a course we called "Communications and Media." We used this course to prove that our home-educated daughter did not suffer from lack of social opportunities!

The most useful broad subject categories were: Science; Math; Language Arts, which includes speech, reading writing, drama, film, etc.; Social Studies, which includes current events, history magazines, books, historical fiction, geography (traveling), biographies, etc.; Creative Arts, which includes music, dance, art, etc.; Physical Education, including sports, walking, biking, swimming; and our invention, Independent Living, which includes anything else, such as shop, home economics, business, computers, typing, jobs, travel arrangements, dining out, etc..

For marking purposes, I would assign a letter for each subject category:

S = Science
LA = Language Arts
M = Math
SS = Social Studies
IL = Independent Living
CA = Creative Arts
PE = Physical Education

Begin by marking the journal with an appropriate subject letter beside each activity (see example). On separate pieces of paper, put a heading for each subject category and separately list the activities from the journal (see example).

Monday

• Made breakfast eggs and muffins (1 hour) IL

- Picked up bedroom (1/2 hour) IL
- Watched talk show on TV (1 hour) SS
- Read newspaper (1/2 hour) SS
- Rode bike to library, read *Popular Science* magazine, started read
  ing *A Separate Peace* (1 1/2 hour) PE, S, LA
- Fixed lunch, baked cookies (1 1/2 hour) IL
- Cleaned hamster cage, walked dog (1 hour) IL or S
- Delivered newspapers (2 hours) IL
- Worked on customer accounts (1/2 hour) M
- Watched movie *Dances with Wolves* (3 hours) LA or SS
- Talked with friends (1/2 hour)
- Practiced trumpet (1/2 hour) CA
- Read more of *A Separate Peace* before bed (1 hour) LA

Tuesday

- Made breakfast, cleaned kitchen (1 hour) IL
- Walked dog, fed hamster (1/2 hour) IL or S
- Apprenticed at garden/nursery—watered plants, restocked
  shelves, carried orders for customers, swept and dusted (3
  hours) IL or S
- Made lunch, cleaned kitchen (1/2 hour) IL
- Read *A Separate Peace* (1 hour) LA
- Wrote letter to material supply catalog from address from
  Popular Science magazine (1 hour) LA
- Practiced basketball with neighbors (1 hour) PE
- Rode bike to store, bought ice cream cone, bubble gum (1/2
  hour) PE and IL
- Delivered newspapers (2 hour) IL
- Ate dinner, talked about war with family (1 hour) SS
- Played Monopoly with family (1 hour) M
- Played with dog and took for walk (1 hour) IL, PE or S
- Read some of *A Separate Peace* before bed (1 hour) LA

Language Arts (1st Page)
Total Hours 6.5 Hours

- Reading *A Separate Peace* 4
- Film *Dances With Wolves* 1.5
- Writing Letter to supply company 1

Social Studies (2nd Page)
Total Hours 4 Hours

- Current Events TV show - creativity 1
- Newspapers .5
- Family discussion 1
- Movie *Dances with Wolves* 1.5

Math (3rd Page)
Total Hours 1.5 Hours

- Newspaper customer accounts .5
- Monopoly game 1

Science (4th Page)
Total Hours 3 Hours

- Daily care of animals 2.5
- *Popular Science* magazine .5

Physical Education (5th Page)
Total Hours 1.5 Hours

- Bike riding .5
- Basketball 1

Independent Living (6th Page)
Total Hours 11.5 Hours

- Daily housekeeping .5
- Cooking activities 4.
- Newspaper job 4.
- Nursery apprenticeship 3.0

Creative Arts (7th Page)
Total Hours .5

- Trumpet practice .5

Total Hours All Subjects 28.5 Hours

This sample is only for two days. Your record-keeping summary should be for one month (or longer) at a time. I chose sample activities that were common activities, not necessarily academic activities. Obviously time spent with a tutor or mentor on Advanced Math would count towards Math credit. For more ideas, issues of *Growing Without Schooling, Home Education Magazine* and *The Teenage Liberation Handbook* by Grace Llewellyn are excellent resources for ideas of ways to "unschool" school subjects. After the first month, it should be possible to figure the average time spent on many activities. For our children, we found their average time on housework to be one hour per day. We no longer recorded this activity, but just gave them credit for the average. We discovered that the average time for reading a book for Kira was approximately 6 hours. After that she just kept track of the names of the books she finished. We knew from our calendar how often she had lessons and activities and how long they took. Journal-writing for this purpose became necessary only to write down unusual activities; often just a notation on the calendar would do.

Putting Together a Transcript

When our son was ready to graduate, our record-keeping system showed that he had six credits in Social Studies. In reviewing the records, we could see that these credits could be renamed Current Events, Geography, American History, World History, etc. We determined this by reviewing the listed activities and his bibliography. His transcript then does not list Social Studies; instead it lists credits in courses that were renamed from his records.

Both children had 5 or 6 credits in Independent Living. In reviewing their records, we saw that we could rename some of these credits Consumer Math, Business Math, Typing I, Career Exploration, Home Economics, Shop, etc. Their transcripts do not say "Independent Living", but list these other classes.

The advantage of classifying activities into broad categories is that it can spare families the frustration of keeping track of many different subjects. It was much easier to reclassify the activities in the broad categories at the end of the record-keeping process. We call this creating an "after-the-fact" curriculum.

But is This Really Worth Credit?

Coming from a traditional academic background, we were incredulous when we were informed by Clonlara that daily activities counted for academic credit. Are the children really learning?, we wondered. Happily, we can see the fruits of this method as our children approach maturity. They both read beautifully and choose excellent books for their enjoyment. Kira has read some Shakespeare, among other classic authors. Andy reads Adam Smith, Homer, Tolstoy, etc. They both can write clearly and sometimes even beautifully. We never required them to write. They chose to write because they eventually had something to express. Now sixteen and eighteen years old, they have practical business and job skills. They have learned compassion and responsibility through caring for family pets. They know what is required to run a house and business well.

In contrast, the National Education Association (NEA) has publicly stated that out of 900 hours of school per year, only 200 are "on task." "On task" means time spent teaching the required subject matter. The rest of the time is spent changing classes, having lunch, getting settled for the start of the class, preparing to leave a class, etc.. Of those 200 hours "on task," how many hours is an individual student actually paying close attention, ready to learn what is being taught? My guess would be that very few students are getting full benefit of those 200 hours "on task." However, high school students are being given credit for 900 hours, when admittedly only 200 are "on task."

As home educators, we can enrich our children's lives with academic and cultural opportunities by staying alert to their interests and suggesting to them additional activities. In our family, our ideas were sometimes welcomed and at other times, ignored. What we tried to convey was our support of and interest in our children's choice of activities. The atmosphere in this type of learning environment has been one of warmth and respect, so different from the atmosphere during school days, when we were constantly worrying and chastising our children for not doing their best by school standards. "Report card" time in our family became a time of appreciation for all the activities completed to date. "Look how many credits you have earned! Look at all the activities you have done!"

What a wonderful difference!

And What About College?

APPENDIX L

Scoring A's In Traditional Courses

In the early 1970's, somehow I managed to get a degree in chemistry at UCLA. I didn't study much, and my grades were mediocre. Returning to college a decade later, I earned a second bachelor's degree in Medical Technology with much better results. Despite the conflicting demands of home and family, I got straight A's in a very demanding program at the University of North Dakota. I do not memorize readily, so this feat is even more remarkable.

I did it by assuming, up front, that I would never have time to study for tests or final examinations. And I never did have time. My approach allowed me to take most tests and finals with an hour of review before the test — certainly no all-night cram sessions.

I always thought my results peculiar to me and my situation and did not see it as applicable to a wider audience until my husband in his mid-30's tried the same tactics in a master's degree program for public health and periodontology. We couldn't believe it. He had never been much of student either, and he was the first person in the program's history to earn straight "A's" the first year.

So, for you homeschoolers attempting traditional academic classes for the first time, I offer this simple, practical method to succeed. You will find this particularly effective for classes that require a great deal of memorization: history, most science classes, geography, economics - any class where you take a lot of notes, have a lot of hand-outs, and have to regurgitate a lot of information. The method also works well for studying for drivers' tests, or any other situation where you have to recall what seems like too much material.

Here are the steps:

1. Take lecture notes on one side only of lined paper. Be as legible and clear as possible; you don't want to have to re-copy these notes! Use a rough outline form; avoid paragraphs. Develop abbreviations for frequently used terms. For example, in medical technology classes, I abbreviated diagnosis as "dx".

2. Use a multi-color pen to take notes and gradually develop a "code," for example green for dates, red for important names in a history class. This makes the notes more interesting to read and enhances recall.

3. Always ask for immediate clarification of confusing points—either during or after the lecture. Do not wait until the day before the test! Include an explanation of the clarification in your notes.

4. Date every lecture note page. And date all handouts. Don't separate them; keep them in one subject binder in chronological order.

5. Take notes on assigned reading. Emphasis here is on lecture notes, so reading notes can be very brief, perhaps just definitions of unfamiliar terms or chapter and section headings or main points. In my experience, if you know the lecture material, you get an "A". Include reading notes in chronological order with lecture notes and handouts.

6. Review every day, six or seven days a week for the entire semester. How? Simply read the notes and handouts from day one. Don't try to memorize, just read. Use a highlighter to add color and interest to important points. Read handouts once, highlighting important points. On subsequent days, just read the highlighted points.

You will start to notice something after 10 or 20 days. Somehow you will know everything on every page, even though you have made no effort to memorize it.

7. Throughout the entire semester, every day review all your notes.

This applies even when the class moves on to a new unit. Always review notes from the first day to the current day.

As the semester progresses, you will notice that you can just skim earlier pages of notes because you have memorized them. Thus, regardless how far you are into the semester and how many notes you have, review for a single class takes ten to twenty minutes per day. Do these reviews in five minute "snatches" throughout the day, and you almost won't know you are studying. If questions come up during a review, get them answered the next day in class.

8. Review all notes for thirty to sixty minutes before major examinations and finals. That's it! Of course, you will still have to devote extra time to researching and writing papers, doing special projects, and so on. But you will not have to worry about cramming for tests.

AFTERWORD

I want to hear from you. Please write with your questions and comments. Also, I would like additional personal accounts of home-schoolers applying to college to include in future editions of this book. Tell me your experiences, good and bad. What other areas does this book need to address?

Cafi Cohen
c/o Holt Associates
2380 Massachusetts Ave.
Suite 104
Cambridge, MA 02140

Email: cfcohen@pacbell.net

Please visit my web page, Homeschool-Teens-College at:

http://www.homeschoolteenscollege.net

And What About College?

Index

COLLEGE INDEX

THE BEGINNER'S GUIDE TO HOMESCHOOLING

Expanded, rewritten, and updated for 2000–2001!

In print since 1995, this book has helped thousands of people explore and start homeschooling. Author Patrick Farenga, with his wife Day, homeschools three girls and publishes *Growing Without Schooling* magazine, the nation's first homeschooling magazine founded by the late John Holt in 1977. Farenga offers his years of experience to provide you with homeschooling advice, support, and resource listings. $10.95 ISBN: 0-913677-17-5 128 pages. Index; bibliography.

"A helpful guide for anyone starting on the homeschooling journey. Chock-full of tips, ideas, and suggestions for resources. Perfect for anyone with questions about homeschooling how-tos. **A great little book!**"—Helen Hegener, *Home Education Magazine*

"*The Beginner's Guide* is **a triumph of common sense**!"—John Taylor Gatto, author of *The Underground History of American Education* and *Dumbing Us Down*

Ask your local bookstore to order these titles, or order directly from Holt/GWS: 888-925-9298 (8AM–5PM, EST); www.holtgws.com

---

AND THE SKYLARK SINGS WITH ME: Adventures in homeschooling and community-based education, by David Albert.

Foreword by Joseph Chilton Pearce.

 A magnificently written tale about how David and his wife took to heart the lesson that to educate a child well is to enable her to find her own destiny. A marvelous example of how children spur adult learning, as well as about how parents can help children learn without always teaching them. A unique homeschooling story, filled with practical wisdom on a wide range of subjects (especially strong on science and nature education) which will reassure families going forth on their own homeschooling adventures.

$16.95 ISBN: 0-86571-401-0 221 pages.

"David Albert gives us, with unpretentious clarity and admirable economy, as profound an insight into the development of intelligence in children as is to be found in many a ponderous professional tome. ...A superb model of what all parents can do to bring forth the best in their children, and share in the joys and riches of doing so."—Joseph C. Pearce

GROWING WITHOUT SCHOOLING. Since 1977 when the late author and teacher John Holt founded GWS, we have been innovators and leaders in exploring how and why children can learn outside of school.

Here are some recent feature articles to give you a sense of what you will read every two months in *Growing Without Schooling:*

- Hard Times at Home: Is Homeschooling Still Possible?
- Young People's History Projects
- Late Readers Turn Out OK
- Rethinking Discipline
- How Parents Are Changed by Homeschooling

GWS also gives you practical ways to help your children learn outside of school, news about the homeschooling movement in the U.S. and abroad, reviews useful books and materials, and helps you connect with others through our Directory of families and organizations. Join us today!

"Many thousands of us are grateful for all the years the *GWS* has provided families the opportunity to share ideas, insight, and support for independent learning and thinking. Over the years *GWS* has won wide respect for plain talk about childhood and family life and has always affirmed John Holt's sincerity of purpose and deep respect for children."— Earl Gary Stevens, ME

"We've reviewed this perennially, because it's the perennially great periodical, review, and resource guide for homeschoolers. Still excellent."—*Millennium Whole Earth Catalog*

US Rates			
1 year	(6 issues)	#2001	$26
2 years	(12 issues)	#2002	$46
3 years	(18 issues)	#2003	$61

**Order directly from
Holt/GWS: 888-925-9298
(8AM–5PM, EST)
www.holtgws.com**
HOLT/GWS, 2380 MASSACHUSETTS AVE.
STE. 104-AW, CAMBRIDGE MA 02140

FOREIGN RATES				
		Surface		Airmail
1 Yr	#2004	US $30	#2008	US $41
2 yrs	#2005	US $54	#2020	US $76
3 yrs	#2006	US $73	#2021	US $106